Investing for Smarties

Investing for Smarties

How to Manage Your Own Portfolio and Keep All the Profits Yourself

William Cubberley

iUniverse, Inc.
New York Lincoln Shanghai

Investing for Smarties
How to Manage Your Own Portfolio and Keep All the Profits Yourself

iUniverse books may be ordered through booksellers or by contacting:

iUniverse
2021 Pine Lake Road, Suite 100
Lincoln, NE 68512
www.iuniverse.com
1-800-Authors (1-800-288-4677)

ISBN-13: 978-0-595-39077-9 (pbk)
ISBN-13: 978-0-595-83466-2 (ebk)
ISBN-10: 0-595-39077-3 (pbk)
ISBN-10: 0-595-83466-3 (ebk)

Printed in the United States of America

CONTENTS

ACKNOWLEDGEMENTS

The first people I want to thank are the incredibly gifted and dedicated professionals who helped me survive a life-threatening illness that began in 1997. I've listed them in the order I encountered them, as it would be impossible to rank them in importance.

Joseph Phillips, M.D. at the Hattiesburg Clinic in Mississippi first diagnosed my problem and has cared for and guided me through the maze to recovery. Gary A. Abrams, and all the following doctors are at the Kirklin Clinic and The University of Alabama Hospital in Birmingham. Dr. Abrams decided what needed to be done to correct my problem. J. Stevenson Bynon, Jr., M.D. is the Director of the Liver and Pediatric Transplant Programs at Kirklin Clinic. He consulted with other doctors and planned my surgery. Devin E. Eckhoff, M.D. performed the transplantation of a donor liver to me. David C. McGiffin repaired my heart during the same operation. And finally, Brendan M. McGuire, M.D., has watched over me in the years following my transplant.

I will always carry a warm spot in my heart, not only for those doctors, but for all the other caring individuals at the Kirklin Clinic, the Hattiesburg Clinic, and the children's surgery ward at UAB Hospital, where I received special and expert care following my surgery. These remarkable individuals have made it possible for me to continue the marvelous experience of life.

I must also mention my wife, Carol, who did so much to help me through the illness. No one could hope for more from a life's partner. She has also been a tremendous help with this book. It would not have been possible without her.

I'd like to thank Jim Martin. Dr. Martin was the Dean of Libraries at the University of Southern Mississippi when I started this book. His encouragement and loan of books from his personal library helped a lot. Thank you, Jim.

My son, Bill, Jr., and my daughter, Hilda Vaughan, each read the manuscript carefully and, from a beginner's point of view, made numerous helpful suggestions and corrections. They provided support and encouragement throughout.

"Employ your time in improving yourself by other men's writings, so that you shall gain easily what others have labored hard for."

—*Socrates*

FOREWORD

Reflecting back over the past forty five years of my investing life, I came to realize how ill prepared I was for what was coming at me. In those days, and even up until the present, we were taught either a trade in an apprenticeship program, or a profession in high school and college. In other words, we were taught how to make money. Little help was available to show young people how to manage their earnings and to invest any excess funds.

As a result of this failure to educate, most beginners either attempt to educate themselves or allow others to make their investment decisions for them. As I found out, both these paths are fraught with danger.

If beginners do not have a solid foundation and a well formulated, proven plan, their funds can be consumed by a sophisticated industry eager to pounce on unwary investors.

With this in mind, I concluded that an easily understood guide was sorely needed: a guide to not only show how to invest, but to warn beginners of the traps that have been set.

With the insights you'll find in this book, you will understand why so few small investors thrive and prosper. You will learn how to avoid the pressures you'll encounter as you experience this deceptively simple-appearing opportunity to better your life.

I wrote this book to encompass an entire lifetime of saving and investing. That time is divided into phases. You could stop at any point and continue investing in that fashion, or you could advance on to more sophisticated methods presented further on. Those decisions can be made as you gain experience in the marketplace and learn how you react. Most importantly, you'll learn how much time and effort you're willing to invest in making the decisions that are critical to your success.

You must be absolutely honest with yourself when deciding how sophisticated your trading life will be. To get involved in an elaborate trading plan and
then get lazy could prove disastrous.

So as you progress through this book, try to realistically identify where you
will be comfortable. If you step into an area that negatively affects you, either
monetarily or emotionally, be quick to recognize your error. Step back and
return to your comfort zone

INTRODUCTION

"If you wait, all that happens is that you get older."

—Mario Andretti, automobile racer

In today's world, the importance of starting early with a well-planned retirement program has never been greater.

Almost every book or article you'll read on planning your financial future will suggest to first consider how much money you'll need to retire comfortably, and to then fund those needs appropriately. Almost all brokers or mutual funds have even gone so far as to design formulas to help beginners reach their goals.

Of course, no one can know how much money will be required to live comfortably forty years in the future. Experts, for instance, cannot predict what inflation will be next week, let alone in the distant future.

When I first started my working life, a fellow worker came to work one day with an article he wanted to share with us. The article predicted that in ten years the average worker in America would be making $11,000 a year. We all agreed that such an eventuality would be great but probably not possible considering that we all were making less than $5,000 per year at the time.

There was no way for us to predict what we would need at the beginning of the 21st century, and there's no way to predict what will be needed forty years from now. So how will you know how much to place in your retirement accounts? It's quite simple. Begin as early as possible with funds you can comfortably afford, and manage your account in an intelligent manner as described in this book. No one will know what's comfortable better than you.

Many years ago when I was first beginning my adult life, an insurance executive visited my workplace. To emphasize why we should begin planning for our future, he quoted an incredible statistic. "Seven out of ten Americans by the time they reach 65 years old will either be dead or dead broke."

Granted, that was many years ago and some may argue the world has changed. Certainly the life expectancy of Americans is longer now than it was forty years ago, which only increases the importance for planning to support your later years. Since the average retiree is expected to live twenty, thirty, or more years after retirement, its imperative to prepare for the impact inflation and medical expenses will inflict on your budget.

According to the Social Security website, without Social Security benefits, half of all Americans over 65 would be destitute. If you're relying on Social Security to support you in your later years you could be in trouble. The government claims you'll be protected because your account will be adjusted for inflation each year. But in 2004 the inflation-adjusted increase was less than the increase in Medicare premiums. Pressures such as these won't go away, further weakening benefits that are already inadequate.

Furthermore, I have not seen any proposed rational solution to the problems Social Security will face when it reaches the point, coming soon with baby boomers reaching retirement age, where there are more individuals collecting than paying into the system.

A currently popular proposed "solution" calls for the privatization or partial privatization of the system. This proposal would allow participants to invest a portion of their contribution themselves, however they choose

Wall Street, I'm sure, is delighted with this idea. To gain access to such a huge amount of wealth must surely have brokers rubbing their hands together and licking their chops. As you'll see, considering the past performance of brokers and mutual funds, future retirees could be in for even more trouble than they now are.

Unfortunately, with lobbyists making huge donations to politicians, there's a good chance partial privatization will be pushed through congress. In that case, the lessons in this book will become even more important.

In the first place, Social Security was only intended to be a safety net, not a full retirement plan. Furthermore, think about how unreliable Social Security is. To begin with, you fund your account with current value dollars, but because of inflation, you're paid back with cheapened dollars. And to add insult to injury, you're taxed on those funds. Worst of all, no one can be sure Social Security will be there for you when you need it. The government knows that Social Security is on shaky ground and some laws have been passed to make it easier for you to rely on your judgment instead of the government's to protect your future. We'll discuss those laws in following pages.

One more thought about Social Security: as long as the government continues stealing (excuse me, "borrowing") from the Social Security "Trust Fund", to "reduce" its deficit, and replacing the funds with I.O.U.s, your Social Security "promise" is in jeopardy. Think about it for a minute. Who will be paying back those I.O.U.s? Of course, the very same workers who will be expected to repeatedly increase their contributions to support all those future long-living retirees. The whole Social Security system is in doubt.

In fact, as recently as August of 2004, Alan Greenspan, the then head of the Federal Reserve, warned that individuals needed to be told that their Social Security fund could be in danger and suggested they make other plans.

These facts are apparently not known to a large segment of our population. If they are, they are not sinking in. According to a telephone poll conducted by Maritz Research:

- 26% of the people called had saved nothing

- 34% had saved less than $25,000

- 11% had saved $25,000 to $49,999

- 10% had saved $50,000–$99,999

- 19% had saved more than $100,000 toward their retirement.

In a later poll conducted by the 2003 Retirement Confidence Survey, sponsored in part by AARP, it was found that most of today's workers feel surprisingly positive about what the future holds. (July/August 2003 issue of *AARP Magazine*.)

According to the article that is not good news. That rosy glow we may be feeling about our future seems to stem from apathy. In other words, sticking our heads in the sand and hoping for the best.

Sarah Zapolsky, AARP senior research adviser, who worked with the Employee Benefit Research Institute and the American Savings Education Council on the survey worries that the comfortable economic future of Americans is in jeopardy.

I have included some additional reading in the bibliography to show how the Social Security Trust Fund has been mismanaged over time. All Americans should be outraged at how our elected officials have quietly trampled on our futures. But we can't place all the blame on them for what happened and is still happening to our retirement system.

We have two major problems with the way our country's fiscal affairs are conducted. One, as long as we reward politicians by reelecting them based on the amount of federal dollars they bring home, we'll never stop the excessive spending that's going on. Two, as long as bureaucrats are paid based on the size of their departments, we'll never stop the bloating of government.

Where did all the statesmen go?

I hope that after reading this book you will begin setting aside a small amount of your earnings toward your future. Doing so will be a giant step toward securing your future financial health. Knowing how to invest those funds will be your next step and what this book is all about.

To be successful over many years is not an easy task if you don't have a well-defined plan for success. The good news is you won't have to be brilliant or worried constantly about your investments.

The methods described in the following pages are exactly the same as the ones used by some of the most successful investors in history.

I wish I would have had the knowledge you are about to discover when I first started my adult life. I could have avoided many mistakes and setbacks.

Many young people have so much self-confidence they believe they will be successful later on and won't need early planning. Besides, they feel, they have plenty of time before getting serious about their financial future. They feel they need all their current earnings for current expenses.

Unless a habit of saving and investing is started early, with the money taken off the top of earnings, many will never quite reach the point where they feel they have enough "extra" to begin. If they begin later, they won't have the time to be patient and let their investments grow, with the result that they may panic and make risky choices.

You may think that investing properly may be just too complicated for you. After all, you could lose all of your money and have nothing to show for your efforts.

The good news is almost anyone can invest successfully. By using common sense, self-discipline, a little effort and the basic rules outlined in this book you could easily retire a millionaire.

This book was designed to show the beginning and unsuccessful investor how to go about addressing this very important part of their future

This book was not written in an academic way with long winded, vague references including lots of graphs, definitions, averages, and fluff which most beginning investors find boring and confusing. It was designed rather as a step-by-step path to success.

I'll include warnings of the pitfalls and traps that have been laid over a long period of time by some very smart people. They're meant to benefit <u>them</u>, not you. After all, for them to become very wealthy, a lot of small investors must feed them with their failures. You will be confronted with many negative forces as you progress through your investing experiences. I will try to address the serious ones and show how to side-step them.

Hopefully, I have convinced you of the importance of saving regularly starting as early as possible and that you will continue reading on. A little effort now could change your life. I promise you, you won't be bored. There's something special about going up against the established financial world and winning. It's easy and you'll enjoy it.

"You miss one hundred percent of the shots you don't take."

—Wayne Gretsky, hockey player

1

THE IMPORTANCE OF BEGINNING EARLY

"Man who waits for roast duck to fly into mouth must wait very, very, long time."

—Chinese proverb

I sympathize with young people when they say "I can't begin to think about investing for my future at this time in my life. I have so many things I need and want."

So be it, but some examples might encourage you to put off a few wants to ensure you will be independent later on.

For instance, if at age 25 you were able to invest $2,000 a year for five years, and then never added to your investments, this is what your account would be worth when you retire at 65, (assuming the stock market's average return of 10%.)

First installment	$ 2,000
First year's earnings at 10%	$ 200
Account value after one year	$ 2,200
Second installment	$ 2,000
Second year's earnings	$ 420
Second year's accumulated value	$ 4,620

Third installment	$ 2,000
Third year's earnings	$ 662
Third year's accumulated value	$ 7,282
Fourth installment	$ 2,000
Fourth year's earnings	$ 928
Fourth year's accumulated value	$10,210
Fifth installment	$ 2,000
Fifth year's accumulated value	$13,431

At this point, you have invested $10,000 and earned $3,431.22. Doesn't look very impressive, does it? However, for the next 35 years you do not add to your account. Just put it aside and do not use any funds. Allow it to generate on its own. When you are ready to use the funds your account will be worth an astounding $377,450.01. That's what compounding can do for you.

Now let's say you decide you don't want to start that early in your life. You have just too many obligations. Fair enough. Let's suppose you decide to wait until the pressure is off, say 20 years until you're 45. Using the same calculations, your retirement account would be worth $56,105.54. Not too shabby, but what a difference from starting earlier.

Now let's see what your account would be worth if you started at 25 with a $2,000 startup and added $2,000 a year for the entire 40 years. The result would be $973,703. Wow! Imagine, you only invested $80,000 and you retire with almost one million dollars. Compounding! It's incredible.

But that's assuming only a 10% growth rate, and that is not what we are aiming for. By correctly using the rules and methods described in the following pages you can very well multiply the above results many times over. The point I'm making here is that compounding is powerful. By changing their lifestyles slightly, most adults can fund their financial future in a meaningful way.

2

THE VERY BEGINNING

"There's not a lot you can do about the national economy but there is a lot you can do about your personal economy."

—Zig Zigler

When you are first starting your investing career you must make some very basic decisions. Protecting your wealth is primary. You may be the perfectly disciplined investor, but you should never forget about all of those very smart people who have designed some very sophisticated ways to enrich themselves. They take advantage of the gullibility and laziness of small investors. I know this sounds harsh, but I have spoken with so many small investors who complain that because of others they have never made any money from their investments. They grouse about how the market is fixed; their broker is stupid; their timing was wrong, etc. There was probably some truth in all of their complaints, but when asked what their plan had been they just blinked. They think for a minute and reply, "Why, just like everyone. I set up a brokerage account and invested as my broker suggested."

After reading this book, I hope you'll realize how dangerous that approach can be. With further questioning, they almost all said they stopped investing in the market because they had lost a considerable amount of their savings. They were embarrassed and ashamed of their losses. They were presently investing in safe places where they wouldn't be outsmarted or cheated.

The best way to avoid all this ugliness is to have a plan, know the pitfalls, and know whom you can trust for guidance. Be diligent, build on your strengths, know your weaknesses and always keep in mind that what you're doing is some pretty serious business. Do it right and you will flourish. Get lazy and watch out!

OK, enough warnings. The first decision you'll need to make is: Whom will I use, or more importantly, whom can I trust to handle my investments? If you don't work for a company that has an in-house retirement plan you'll need to buy company stocks directly from the companies, buy mutual funds, or set up a brokerage account. They all have their good and bad qualities.

Buying shares directly from a company will save a brokerage commission, and you can set up a dividend reinvestment plan with them. This will allow all your earned dividends to automatically be reinvested in more stock. However, if you decide to sell the shares back to the company it can take time to get your money. I suggest not buying shares direct from companies. When you have finished this book you'll understand why it's not wise to fall in love with a company.

Buying directly from a mutual fund is okay if you buy as I suggest. If you buy a mutual fund from most brokers, a no-load mutual fund will pay the brokerage commission instead of you. But even on no-load funds, somebody pays the piper, but that's another story that I'll explain later.

Setting up an account with a broker is probably a good idea. When choosing a broker, you'll need to weigh the benefits of each.

A full service brokerage house should be avoided like the plague.

In the chapter "Choosing a broker" I explain why I have such strong feelings on this matter.

I suggest using an online discount broker. If you decide to go this route, you can buy your investments through them. They will hold your stock certificates and funds for you, keep your books for you, send you monthly statements and an annual 1099 form, and make available to you all the sophisticated analysis they pay big bucks for. All this may not be free of charge, so check to be sure. There will be a small commission when you buy or sell. Most importantly, their brokers will not be bothering you. For the low commissions they charge, you will not receive any guidance on where or how to invest.

Believe me, brokerage guidance is something a new investor does not need.

However, you may need help setting up your individual retirement plan, and that is a service a discount broker will provide. They will send you the forms and walk you through them if needed There are a number of discount brokerages. I use T.D. Waterhouse occasionally, because I can trade international stocks more easily with them. Since I advise beginners not to buy foreign stocks this will not be important at first. Waterhouse or any one of many other brokerage houses will serve you fine. What you'll be looking for are low commission rates and excellent research tools that are easy to use and understand. Choose three or four and play around with them online. There's more about this in Chapter 3. If you're not clear on something, call them up and ask questions. They are usually very understanding and helpful.

When my niece was trying to familiarize herself with online investing she called her broker and spent two hours with them. She said the total experience was positive. Not once did they appear to be anxious to be rid of her. In fact, the last thing they said to her was "If you have any other questions please do not hesitate to call. That's why we're here and thank you for using us." That's what I call customer service, and that's what you should be looking for. If they will bend over backward to help you when you're starting, that will be a good indicator of how much you can depend on them later.

Once you've chosen a broker, request an application and sign up. If you're computer literate you can do that online. The next step will be to fund your tax-sheltered account. (More on this later.) You can send them a check or you could have your bank send them a prearranged amount each month the same as if they were paying a bill for you. Most brokers will place those funds into a money market fund automatically, where you're contributions can be earning interest until you have sufficient funds to begin investing properly. Granted, you won't earn much, but your funds will be safe and moving in the proper direction. Some brokerages do not pay interest on the funds in your account, so be sure to find out before signing up.

The next decision to make is: How am I going to protect my fledgling account and all of my future earnings from Uncle Sam? If you work for a company that has a human resources department they can and will help you through the maze. If, however, your company does not have such help or if you're self-employed, you'll need to decide a vehicle to use that achieves tax efficiency for your particular situation.

Now that you've set up and begun funding your account, and decided how you'll protect it from the Internal Revenue Service, there will be one more important task for you. This last task is the one most people find very difficult.

That is to protect your funds from yourself. You shouldn't feel free to dip into your account for every little desire or for every cockamamie investment scheme you'll run into as you move along. In fact, I suggest that for the first three to five years you leave your investments in a money market fund or any other interest-bearing account. When you have sufficient savings to meet their requirements, buy into a top notch, low cost, total market index fund such as Vanguard Total Stock Market Index Fund. In that way you'll avoid silly mistakes until your funds are sufficient to allow you to diversify your portfolio and trade stocks in an intelligent and time proven fashion.

I once knew a man who was a co-pilot working for Eastern Airlines. The joke at Eastern was that the first five years you flew for them your job was to be careful not to fall out of your chair and to be able to land the plane in case the pilot had a heart attack. In fact, he told me that the very first flight he made for them the pilot introduced himself and said, "Don't touch anything unless I tell you to." I have the same feelings regarding investing. If you decide to venture outside the confines of the suggested practices presented in this book before you understand the markets, you could be jeopardizing your entire financial future. Meanwhile, you'll be gaining the smarts to enable you to discern between excellent opportunities and absurd ones.

One of the silliest bits of advice I've read, presented by supposedly intelligent individuals, is that a person can take more chances with their investments when they are young because they have a long time to recover from mistakes. I suggest that is the worst bit of advice a beginner should hear for two reasons. First, is that each dollar you invest in the beginning, through compounding, has the potential to grow over time to multiple thousands of dollars if properly invested.

Second, in the beginning when a person is training, if he falls for every harebrained idea he encounters, he could be set back seriously or even permanently. Usually these questionable insights come from individuals trying to sell dangerous products such as commodity futures or options. These are places beginners should not be. These dangerous investments offer only one advantage for beginners: excitement.

Beginners are usually young, and young people are often looking for quick results. With exaggerated belief in their abilities, and lack of experience, they fall prey to overblown false claims from many sources. I receive, on average, ten such claims in the mail each week. One claimed that by investing $10,000 and by using his guidance I could turn that initial investment into $100,000 in one year. This is very tempting for a novice. To draw you in more, they claim they will return your money if you are not completely satisfied. Not the money you will probably lose, but usually only a prorated portion of the unused issues. Investment newsletters are a huge business. Let's face it. If they were that wonderful, wouldn't they just be investing themselves? You certainly do not need those hucksters cluttering up your mind with their exaggerated claims of success and their hidden shortcomings. I suggest tossing them in the wastebasket without opening them so as not to be tempted. These companies/individuals are very good at selling and that could be dangerous for you. I am constantly amazed by how a person who may find it difficult to lend $20 to a colleague will turn around and send hundreds of dollars to a perfect stranger. Okay, enough of that.

So far you have set up a tax sheltered brokerage account and begun funding that account in a manner of your choosing. You have instructed your broker to place your funds in an interest bearing account such as a money market account, and when you had sufficient funds you have moved on to a broad market index mutual fund. You now have the time to learn about how to have a successful investing career. By using the sources and methods I suggest, you will know all you'll need to know. It won't be that hard and you will be surprised at how much fun it will become when everything begins to work. There is a definite feeling of pride in knowing you have stepped into a very tough world and performed with the best of them. Knowing whom you can trust and how to perform with their help is presented in the following chapters.

3

CHOOSING A BROKER

The first cause of failure for most investors is themselves. The second is brokers. What I say here is only intended to protect beginners. By understanding how a broker operates you will be on your guard and can proceed safely.

I got my first insight into how treacherous the market can be for an inexperienced investor back in 1960. A colleague, Alex, received a large inheritance from the estates of his two spinster aunts. The estates included a beautiful house in Coral Gables, Florida, and several hundred thousand dollars worth of bonds and securities. The sisters obviously were two smart investors. The inheritance in today's dollars would be valued at several million dollars.

As you can imagine, Alex was walking on air, very excited and happy about his good fortune. The brokers who had handled his aunts' accounts convinced him that he could do much better by trading stock than with those stodgy ol' bonds. He agreed with them and turned his entire account over to them to trade as they felt best.

For the next three months, Alex walked around with a *Wall Street Journal* in his back pocket, wanting to talk about the market to anyone he could corner. We soon scattered whenever we saw him coming.

Then we noticed that the *Wall Street Journal* and the smile disappeared. In two years, everything was gone. Alex never spoke about what happened; I learned about it from his wife one day at a company picnic.

Those brokers were very good at building greed and trust in the mind of their client. They managed to lose in two or three years what took those two bright ladies a lifetime to accumulate. And all for the commissions they generated by actively trading his account.

Most beginners entering the market believe that brokers will direct them toward a shining future. After all, brokers have studied diligently, have worked hard, and have experience and a huge company's research abilities supporting them.

First, let's look at experience. Most beginners feel that a broker who has been involved in "the market" for ten or twenty years has learned a lot about profiting from the market. This broad experience should enable them to guide you towards a successful investing life. After all, you may think, the more successful you become the more business you will do with them. You both, therefore, can and will prosper.

Actually, what your broker's experience has taught him is how to sell his company's products better. If brokers were honest and straightforward with their clients they would admit they do not know what the future holds any more than a car salesman knows what makes his products run.

Next let's look at diligent study. Most brokers study very hard to pass the tests to become licensed brokers. Aspiring brokers are usually hired on as assistants to brokers. All day long they are required to make "cold calls" from a list of leads obtained from sources by their companies. If a likely person is contacted this person will be turned over to the broker to push the product *du jour*. During these trying times the nascent brokers will be studying very hard to pass the tests to become qualified brokers. Some take months, some quick studies less. Anyway, they work very hard at this, because they hate making all of those calls. Who wouldn't?

Once brokers pass these requirements, most of their studies will center around how to converse with clients. They will spend weeks taking turns role-playing the client or being the all-knowing "investment adviser". Once the broker's company is confident he or she has achieved polished communication skills the new broker will begin honing these skills towards what he or she has been hired to do—buy and sell a lot of stocks! Brokers make their livings on commissions. As you are a novice investor, there's a good chance that a new broker with no experience will be assigned to your account. Just imagine, someone with little more knowledge than you have will be guiding your financial future if you allow it. The more they can legally trade your account, the bigger steaks they will eat and the brighter they will appear to their bosses.

Let's look at the brilliance of brokers for a moment. Oh, they are far from dumb. They are very good at what they do. Like all good salespeople, brokers are mostly personality people. They will listen to your stories, laugh at your jokes, and agree with your philosophy on just about anything. But their main objective is to trade your account. To allow a broker to handle your financial future is like the old story of allowing the fox to guard the henhouse.

A major problem many beginning investors have is trading on advice from their brokers so as not to offend them. After all, the investor may feel he has a friend who is working on his behalf and does not wish to appear rude by rejecting the friend's suggestions. If you are ever confronted with this temptation, forget your better breeding. Save your manners for less risky situations. You're not being nice, you're just being easy. No one can help you out of the mess you most assuredly will find yourself in if you listen to those pitchmen/women.

All of this may seem too rough and coarse for your sensitive nature, but if you're going to involve yourself in this market you had better be prepared for what you will be dealing with. Don't concern yourself about hurting anyone's feelings. Brokers are thick-skinned and your straightforward manner will probably be respected. If not, so what? Call me a grouch if you like, but I have seen many beginning investors financially wiped out, their spirits broken never to return. I have seen broken marriages, nervous breakdowns, heart attacks, and even suicides caused by the excessive pressure that results from foolish trading. Back before online investing I always made it clear to a new broker that I wanted no help and they always respected my wishes.

The only way I know to place you on your guard is to present this market in a blunt straightforward manner. If you ignore these warnings, you haven't a chance.

This brings me to a couple of rules you'll need when dealing with a broker. The first rule is, never visit your brokerage house. They are just too good at doing what they do: selling. You might be tempted to make a move you could later regret. The tape running the latest equity prices across the walls, people shouting instructions across the room, secretaries scurrying about, latest hot tips blurting out over the loud speakers—all these things create excitement. One can only imagine the revenues generated around the world by a hot tip announced by an analyst or guru. I'm amazed at how the atmosphere in these places resembles that of a gambling casino or a carnival.

The second rule is, if you aren't computer literate and must talk to a broker, never ask their advice on investing. If you use the instructions presented in this book and do your homework you won't need any help. In this case two heads definitely are not better than one.

For these reasons I would suggest you set up your trading account with a good online discount brokerage firm. If you are not connected to the Internet you can still place your orders by phone, or you can get online access in your public library.

The website at www.dfin.com will supply you with a list of online discount brokers. The list I'm looking at now has 69 firms listed. Included are their web addresses and general information phone numbers. I've listed four to get you started:

Accutrade.com, 800–494–8939
Offers trades up to 1,000 shares for $29.95 with free research.

Ameritrade.com, 800–454–9272
Offers Internet trades for $10.99, interactive voice response trades for $14.99, broker-assisted trades for $24.99 market, $29.99 limit. Account maintenance is $15 per quarter.

Etrade.com, 800–786–2575
Offers trades for $9.99. In order to maintain eligibility, 27 trades each quarter required.

Scottrade.com, 800–619–7283
Offers online market orders for $7, touchtone limit orders for $12, broker-assisted trades for $17.

The above examples show the importance of reading all the small print in the websites, rather than just choosing a broker from an online pop-up offering "trades for $4". Of course the numbers in the examples listed above are not carved in stone, but were correct at some point in time. Prices and companies are constantly changing, so be sure when choosing an online broker than your information is current.

There is one other matter about brokers that needs to be discussed. After you have become an active investor it will seem like everyone in the world will know about it. You will be overwhelmed with what's known in the trade as "cold calls". When you begin receiving these bothersome calls you'll know your name has been bought from a financial magazine or newspaper you have subscribed to, or from someone from whom you have requested information. The callers' sole purpose is to get your business and they are relentless. Hopefully, with the new national no-call list, this problem will end. If you haven't already signed up, you should at:
http://www.ftc.gov/bcp/conline/edcams/donotcall/index.html

The Waltons invited their new neighbors over to dinner. During dinner Mr. Walton was asked what he did for a living. Eight-year-old Brian Walton jumped in and said "Daddy is a fisherman."

Mrs. Walton gasped "Brian, why do you say that? Your daddy is a stockbroker, not a fisherman!"

"No, Mom. Every time we visit dad at work and he hangs up the phone he laughs, rubs his hands together and says 'I just caught another fish.'"

4

PITFALLS

Take on the Street by Arthur Levitt and Paula Dwyer states that during Levitt's tenure as chairman of the Securities and Exchange Commission (SEC) he had extreme pressures applied to him whenever the SEC tried to have legislation passed by Congress that would protect the investing community. Every time they tried to correct a blatant flaw in the law regarding either company governance, accounting practices, brokerage firms' activities, or others, they were threatened and told to back off. The people hired to lobby for the investing companies would go straight to our representatives and ask them to have the SEC drop the issue. The powerful elected officials, who incidentally had their election campaigns financed by the groups trying to squash the SEC's efforts, would comply by threatening to slash the SEC's budget if they persisted.

What Levitt and Dwyer say next should be of utmost importance to you. They said "Everybody in the financial business has a lobbyist in Washington except the small investor."[1] The only protections the small investors have are the small underfunded agencies which were devised for your protection. The result of this mischief has been damaging to our markets and to the reputation of our business community worldwide.

Many investors have become less trusting and more cynical. Perhaps that's good, but certainly a bitter learning experience. What investors should have learned during the past six years is that they need to pay much more attention

---

1. Levitt, Arthur with Paula Dwyer. *Take on the Street: What Wall Street and Corporate America Don't Want You to Know: What You Can Do to Fight Back.* New York: Pantheon Books, 2002.

to their investments and not allow others to do it for them. Later on I'll explain some short cuts to make the job less time-consuming and less boring.

The main thought to remember is that scoundrels have always been around and always will be. Governments almost always bring about protective measures after the fact. In the meanwhile, many investors are harmed, and no matter how many protective rules are put in place there will be those who will work very hard to develop ways around them.

This brings me to a story of an experience I had in 1974. I had just walked into my broker's office when I was approached by another investor I knew well. He was extremely agitated and wanted me to join a class action suit against the brokerage company whose offices we were standing in at the time.

It seems his fury was brought about by what had just happened that morning. A company the brokerage had been touting had suddenly collapsed without warning. The said company was involved in the oil exploration and development business. Their major area of development had hit rock so hard they could not break through the impenetrable layer.

This was a small company and such news was devastating to them. Oh, the oil was there, they just couldn't get to it. Certainly this was an unforeseen development and something that happens in such businesses. My fellow investor, however, felt that it was our broker's duty to keep track of the company and warn us of any developments, good or bad.

I then told him I could not enter into the lawsuit because of my investment philosophy. I explained to him that I believed the monitoring of my investments is my responsibility and that *I do not trust anyone to do it for me.* I believe this is a grownup's game and should be treated as such. Although it would be good business for a broker to warn me of such events, it's not something I should depend on or expect. Unless a broker commits a criminal act against me I'll take my lumps and move on. My fellow investor, after hearing this, just walked away shaking his head, still steaming.

Another investor that was eavesdropping on us said "I would hate to be you." I hardly knew this person and couldn't figure out what had brought on this attack. After recovering from the first blow, I asked, "How's that?" She replied, "I was just listening to your conversation with that man and I feel that if you do not trust anyone any more than you do you should not be involved in investing or any other business." She was clearly upset with me and I felt it wise not to continue the discussion. I decided to chalk the experience up to a lack of experience on this person's part and left. One thing for sure, that day was not starting out on a happy note.

About six weeks later, while shopping, I came upon the very same person who had admonished me. She looked absolutely awful. She asked if I had time to talk with her in private.

Over a cup of coffee she told of a tragic set of events, not uncommon, which had befallen her. Her broker had convinced her to make two very dangerous moves. He urged her to short several contracts of live cattle, and then to pyramid using the profits from her position. When finally the market turned against her she panicked and shouted across the room, "Sell those cattle contracts of mine." She then left to recover from a most unnerving experience, while her broker did exactly what she told him to do.

Now, because she did not have any long positions the sell order automatically doubled her short position. She didn't return to the brokerage for a while, but eventually the broker called to ask what she wanted to do with her cattle position. She said, "I have no cattle position." When she finally realized what had happened and before she could get out she had lost her entire family's savings and owed the broker almost twenty thousand dollars more. He wanted the money and she didn't have it. She said her husband was threatening to divorce her and take their two boys.

While she was telling me this terrible story she was trying to drink a cup of coffee. Her hands were shaking so badly I was concerned she would drop the coffee. When I suggested that she might have some legal recourse, she brushed the thought aside. She said she had no money to hire a lawyer and her job right now was to try to save her marriage. "Besides," she said, "the experience has shaken me so much that I just want to be shed of it."

This is a tragic story, but a good example of how dangerous this market can be if you do not know how to protect yourself. This is but one unfortunate result of not paying attention.

Just a small mistake and you could be seriously harmed. I'm not attempting to frighten anyone away from investing in securities. I feel that stocks are the best way for a person to build wealth. Knowing what to do by definition will help eliminate the wrong things to do.

"See this glass of water? I mixed it myself. Two parts H, one part O. I don't trust anybody."

5

MUTUAL FUNDS

Earlier I advised you to begin saving in the Vanguard Total Stock Market Index Fund until you have enough money to diversify your own portfolio. Vanguard is just one of many mutual funds, and now we're going to investigate just what mutual funds are, how they work, and their shortcomings.

To begin with, let's go to what a mutual fund is. A mutual fund is a company that buys stock (shares) of other companies. Or they can buy bonds, or real estate, or a number of other investments. An investor who buys units in a mutual fund is actually buying a small piece of everything a mutual fund owns. By doing so a small investor with not much money can diversify and thus lessen the chance of losing all of his money if a company goes bankrupt and he/she only owned shares in that one company. Each fund is described by what type of investments they own, i.e. small capitalization (known as small caps), large caps, bonds, futures, and many, many more. You can choose a socially responsible fund that doesn't invest in tobacco companies and avoid companies that have been accused of polluting or unfair labor practices. Investors are thus able to buy into a fund that they are most comfortable with.

For instance, if you don't feel comfortable with aggressive investing, or if you do, or if you like real estate, etc. etc., there will be a fund suited to your tastes. With over fifty thousand mutual funds worldwide, you shouldn't have a problem finding one to suit you. You may wonder, "How in the world will I know which one is best for me?" There are companies that evaluate mutual funds. A good example would be *Morningstar.com.* But be forewarned, all funds are not as they appear. As you will understand when you have finished this chapter, with the exception of Vauguard's Total Market Index Fund I don't think much of most mutual funds in existence.

Now that we know what mutual funds are, let's look at why and how people use them. Mutual funds are the way that most people save for their later years. The only reasons I can think of to explain their popularity are that investors:

> lack self-confidence;
> are lazy;
> are gullible;
> don't realize how much they are paying their mutual funds.

Now those reasons may explain why individuals are so easily manipulated, but what about those supposed expert retirement fund managers for large companies, municipalities, and teaching systems? They make huge salaries and should know better, yet they invest the funds in their care heavily in mutual funds.

It has been suggested that by investing in mutual funds, the company retirement fund directors can blame the mutual funds for poor performance and so not leave themselves open to being sued by the employees.

I suspect the reason is that that is the way things have always been done and that is the way they have been trained. After all, the status quo seems so logical. If you buy a mutual fund, you have basically hired, for a supposed small fee, experts to direct your retirement funds toward the best vehicles so that you will prosper.

Recently, however, the light is beginning to appear over the heads of some state fund directors. They are beginning to realize how much of a drag owning actively managed mutual funds has been for them.

It may seem harsh to portray investors as unknowing, lazy, gullible, lacking in confidence, but I am convinced these statements are true for the following reasons: I have asked many people why they like mutual funds and have basically received about the same answers. Sometimes I receive just a shrug of the shoulders, but mostly the answer goes something like this, "I buy a mutual fund because it's easy. I give them my money and they use their expertise to direct my funds to the best place for me to make the most from them. I purchase this expertise as I would for any service I need from fixing my car to doing my taxes. What I'm doing is paying a small fee for them to do something I don't know how to do or have the time for."

But people with this attitude, if questioned further, show how little they really know about with whom they have entrusted their entire financial futures. For instance, when asked how much they were paying their mutual funds, most could only guess about how much. The ones who thought they knew mentioned the number they read in their fund prospectus, somewhere around 2%. In quick defense they often blurt out "I certainly don't mind paying such a small amount in exchange for their expert guidance."

But if asked, "2% of what?" they usually just blink. You see, most investors think they're paying 2% of the profit. In reality they're paying *2% of their entire account value every year*. If a mutual fund, for instance, earns 8% and they charge you 2% you will be paying *more than 25% of the funds earnings*. In other words, on a $1,000 investment, your earnings of 8% would equal $80. Your investment would increase to $1080 momentarily, but then the 2% charge of $21.60 (2% of $1080) would be deducted, leaving you with $1058.40.

Now let's look at even worse scenarios. Suppose your fund only earns 4%. They will be taking more than 50% of the earnings. Even worse than that, suppose your fund breaks even or loses money. They still take their 2% for their dubious expert management. If a mutual fund is managing a billion dollars for their clients, which many do, and some much more, a 2% management fee comes to 20 million dollars a year just to service the account. But wait, that's *after* their costs of running the fund. All of those costs, of which there are many, are subtracted first from the gross earnings (which may be boasted of in glossy ads in investment magazines as being 17% or higher) and then the fund subtracts their management fees.

In fact, I recently read that some funds were raising their charges because their clients accounts had dwindled so much the funds couldn't make enough to cover the fund's expenses. Also, because they had been doing such a miserable job, many investors had pulled their money out of the funds while they still had something left. Can you imagine, *the mutual fund will charge their remaining clients more because the fund lost their money?*

Now let's look at some of those hidden costs you will be paying when you own a mutual fund. I think the biggest misconception about mutual funds concerns so-called "no-load" funds. Investors unwittingly believe that buying a no-load mutual fund means you won't be paying a commission to a broker.

First of all, you should understand no one does anything on Wall Street for nothing. You may not pay the broker up-front yourself, but that broker *will* be paid. Your mutual fund will pay him or her, and that is one of the hidden costs your fund will be removing from your account as long as you own it. In fact, in some cases your broker will not only receive his or her sales commission (usually around 4%) but will also receive a lesser amount every year for as long as you own that mutual fund. Imagine, if you buy into a mutual fund and hold it for your entire life, even into retirement, that broker is going to be riding on your financial back.

Another big chunk of your fund's earnings is eaten up by analysts. Because fund managers are portrayed as such superstars in the media, I used to think they were the ones making the decisions. In reality, mutual funds pay millions of dollars to analysts to tell them which stocks to own.

Because fund managers are such nervous nellies, they trade their portfolios much more aggressively than you would need to, producing huge tax and transaction costs.

And what about advertising? You have probably seen those double page spreads in newspapers and magazines, and all of those commercials on the financial news channels. All of that advertising costs a fortune and comes off the top of the fund's earnings.

These are some of the largest costs mutual funds generate; costs you will not have if you direct your own financial life.

Let's suppose you go to a real estate broker and you ask him to sell your house. He says "Sure. We will sell your house for you and we'll charge you 6% commission for doing so." He is successful. He finds a buyer for you and you all go to the settlement to transfer ownership. While looking over the paperwork you notice your broker has charged you, not the 6% agreed upon, but 25%. Astonished, you ask him how come. He explains that the 6% was before their expenses. He explains that he has had considerable expenses while trying to sell your house and has had to add those charges to the 6% originally agreed upon. At that point you would probably pitch a fit and storm out. How long do you think your greedy realtor would stay in business using those deceitful practices? Probably not long. Still mutual funds have been using that very same tactic since their inception. It's just that they are much better at hiding those costs. Buried deep in their annual reports, in footnotes and many different places, is listed everything they have been up to that year. Everything is listed somewhere in that report so as to be totally legal and compliant to all requirements. But as with anything composed by lawyers, the average person can't fathom what it all means. So they toss the report aside and accept what they've been given. The amazing thing to me is

> that millions of investors will accept those small returns their entire lives, never considering that they could do better, much better.

It boggles the mind to consider the millions of investors worldwide who have not caught on to how they are being used. You see, mutual funds have evolved into one of the most profitable vehicles in history for a small group of very slick insiders. Over time, some very smart individuals have figured out the formula to allow themselves to become incredibly wealthy using the money of millions of small investors. By convincing those investors that the mutual fund directors are all-knowing and can do a much better job of investing their life savings, they are therefore entitled to gobble up half or more of any profits generated.

If you decide that you need someone to hold your hand, whether it be a mutual fund or a full service broker, you should be prepared to pay dearly. Try to keep in mind that you're only doing this thing (life) one time and life flies by fast. Developing and executing a well-planned financial life is not that difficult. Doing so early, if possible, is what it's all about. And mutual funds are not a way to do it.

I suppose the reason mutual funds have survived for so long is because there have not been very many scandals in the industry. Oh there have been instances where fund managers have emptied the coffers and fled to South America. These isolated events were not generally widely reported and people soon forgot. However, by the end of 2003 a whole new can of ugly worms had been opened. Accusations concerning fraudulent activities involving some of the largest, oldest, and most respected funds in America were beginning to surface. It appears that owners, managers, their families, and their cronies have benefited from shady shenanigans to downright illegal activities perpetrated against their investors.

For the aforementioned reasons and these latest revelations I would suggest to anyone starting out, or to any investor for that matter, to avoid all actively managed mutual funds. Mutual funds have developed too many ways to skin you.

The point I'm making here is that mutual funds, even those few run in an honest and aboveboard manner, come in a far second to managing your finances yourself, for the following reasons:

1. you won't need a board of directors;

2. you won't be advertising as funds do;

3. you won't be paying any taxes on earnings (capital gains or income taxes);

4. you won't be paying any analysts to help you choose which securities to own;

5. you will be able to invest in any opportunity that presents itself (most funds can not);

6. you won't have to keep a percent of your funds idle in a cash account for redemptions as mutual funds are required by law to do;

7. you won't need a huge office complex with all of the horrific costs that go along with it;

8. last and most important, you won't need an excessively paid fund manager. *You can be the excessively paid manager.*

You will need only an occasional trip to your local library, a few books that I'll recommend, a plan, some study to develop investing skills, and some self confidence. Yes, you will have to do some work to stay on top of your plan but it won't be so difficult. I promise you, fund managers aren't that brilliant.

Many would strongly disagree with what I've said, citing success stories from the past. True, a few superstars have produced incredible returns for their investors. Some attribute their successes to pure genius while others claim that luck had a lot to do with it, i.e. being in the right place at the right time. Maybe their successes were pure genius but I would ask, "how do you know who those future superstars are going to be?"

You could waste years trying to find another success story to latch onto, bouncing around from one fund to another. And all the while having those back end load fees nibble away at your account balance until you're disillusioned to a point of total frustration and disgust.

Earlier I mentioned those advertisements in financial publications where a mutual fund will claim, for instance, a 17% yearly total return for the past five years. This gives the impression that investors received a 17% profit on their accounts for the past five years. Unfortunately those very impressive numbers, as it turns out, are gross profits before overhead, taxes, and of course their management fees. Most investors apparently just see those numbers and think, "Man, I'll be a multi-millionaire when I retire!"

If you are tempted to invest with a particular fund, do yourself a favor first. Call the fund and tell them your intentions. Ask them to send you their investor's packet. In it you will find out how much you'll really be earning—or maybe you won't. You see, they are very good at hiding costs. If you can't find what you're looking for, call them back and tell them you're confused. Tell them you can't figure out how much you would have made if you had owned their fund for the past five years.

If you can't get satisfactory answers, skip it and move on to some other fund or investment. There is presently a movement in Washington to clean up the mutual fund industry. Looking back at past attempts, however, I do not hold out much hope of success. There are just too many lobbyists fighting change. If, however, you follow my advice to not buy mutual funds, you won't need to make decisions concerning who you can trust to be straightforward and honest with you.

The more hands that touch your money between the bank and you, the less chance you have of getting it.

This is a saying from the construction business. The same holds true for investors. If an investor decides to include consultants, mutual funds, and full service brokers in his financial life, the less chance he will have for success.

6

THE PLAN

As the old saying goes, "There are many ways to skin a cat." As you progress through your investing life you may find ways to improve on what I'm about to share with you. You may discover that you are more comfortable with less aggressive investments, or you may not want to work as hard at managing your portfolio, or you may want to work harder at it.

I do not function well under pressure, therefore the plan I will lay out for you is what is comfortable for me; a well researched, moderately aggressive and carefully monitored style. By knowing whom you can trust for your research, your investment choices will be quick and easy. Although choosing and buying the correct investments at the proper time is of utmost importance, you will need to do much more to ensure a successful financial life. As you will see further on in this book, knowing what to buy is no more important than knowing when to sell those very same investments.

To buy and hold a stock for your entire working life for retirement, college expenses, your estate, or other plans is not what will make you super successful. The investing process presented here is the best way to enrich your future in the safest way I know.

7

PROTECTING YOUR NEST EGG

The first decision you'll need to make is how and where to protect your portfolio from Uncle Sam. I have spoken to some people who actually feel guilty about searching out a way to avoid taxes. They say it's un-American to not support their country. I think those well-meaning individuals should consider that if people use the laws Congress has passed to enable them to build wealth, the country will be better off for it.

So, how do we do this? There are several vehicles you can use depending upon your circumstances. If you work for a company that has an in-house retirement plan that matches your contributions, you should definitely investigate that first. Under a traditional 401(k) plan you won't pay taxes on any contributions you or your employer set aside for your retirement. Nor will you pay taxes on your account earnings until you retire and begin drawing from your account.

If you're just starting work in a company you should take the time to find out all about what the retirement plan offers, how it's implemented and what choices you have. For instance, how much can you contribute, what percent matching funds does your company contribute? In what form is the match? If it's company stock, how long must you hold the shares before you can exchange them for another form of investment? It's not a good idea to place your salary and your retirement under the control of the same entity.

Most importantly, how are your funds invested, and how successful have those choices been over time? If your company will allow it, I suggest placing your funds in a broad market index fund such as the Vanguard Total Stock Market Index Fund.

If you do not work for a company that has a 401(k) plan available, or if you work for yourself, you should start an Individual Retirement Account (IRA) as soon as you can afford one. These accounts offer the same benefits as 401(k)s except, of course, no one will be matching your contributions.

You will need to decide which IRA you will contribute to. Of the options available, my number one choice is a Roth. You won't receive tax relief as you contribute to your fund, but the taxman will never have his hand out afterwards. That's right, when you begin drawing funds from your account at retirement, no one will get any of it. Never. You can even pass your Roth on upon your demise, tax free.

Another advantage of a Roth is that any time you should need funds for any reason, you can use any funds you have contributed in the past without any tax implications. You paid the tax up front. Now that applies only to the funds you have contributed. Any earnings from your contributions must stay in your account until age 59½. Of course, if you really *must* have those funds earlier you can have them. It's your money. You'll just have to pay taxes and penalties for early withdrawal.

Conventional IRAs work differently. All contributions, in this case, are removed from your gross earnings each year before calculating your taxes. You will not pay taxes on any earnings until retirement. Unlike a Roth, the funds you withdraw from your account will be taxed according to the tax bracket you are in at that time. In other words, all of your contributions and earnings will be taxed as you use them.

That is why I like a Roth. You may have been taxed on your contributions, but that's not where it will hurt. Let's say you contribute $3,000 a year for 35 years. All told, you will contribute $105,000 over your working life. The taxes you'll pay per year on those contributions using a Roth will depend on your individual situation, ranging from $450 at 15% to $1,050 at 35%, the current top rate as this is written.

Let's say, for example, that your tax situation places you somewhere between the two. Say your $3,000 contribution will cost you, in this hypothetical case, $800 a year to own a Roth IRA instead of a conventional IRA. So for a total of $28,000 in taxes in this case you will never pay taxes on your contributions again, or on your earnings ever. This is to me, and should be to you also, a bonanza. Because if you properly manage your account, the earnings will be huge compared to your contributions.

If you decide to go it alone you'll need a place to do business. By this, I mean a brokerage house. They have the forms you'll need to set up your IRA and will help you fill in the forms properly. Try to keep reminding yourself that what you're doing is some very important stuff. You're laying the foundation for your financial future. The brokerage house is where you can set up and fund your IRA and place your buy and sell orders.

All brokerages in the United States are insured to protect you. You can therefore rest assured that in the event your chosen brokerage house should go broke, your funds and equities are protected. So safety is not a problem, but some other issues should be investigated such as:

> Commission charges
> Annual fees
> Inactivity fees
> Length of wait to reach a representative by phone

Once you've chosen a broker and experienced how they operate, you may decide to try another if you have problems such as:

> Mistakes are made
> Mistakes are not easily corrected
> Lack of courtesy and helpfulness when you have problems.

With all of this accomplished let's move on to how to begin investing.

8

SECOND PHASE

Let's say you have completed your apprenticeship. You have added funds to your account for three to five years. You have studied and are confident you know enough to begin buying and monitoring individual stocks. When you become the part owner of a company you will begin to learn some important things about yourself.

You may learn that the stress of allowing someone else to manage your money is more than you can bear. When you buy a company's stock you're saying, "Okay, Mr. CEO and board of directors, I'm putting my faith in all of you to do a good job." If, however, you are not able to do so and you find you're constantly worried about "what they're up to", you may not be built to withstand the uncertainties of steering your own investment "ship". After all, your health is primary, and there's nothing wrong with retreating back to owning the Vanguard Total Stock Market Index Fund that has brought you this far. You haven't lost the battle. You're just not on the front lines.

If, however, you find that you're comfortable with personally directing your financial future; if you find the whole experience challenging, exciting, and fun, then the rest of this book is for you. Learning how to buy and monitor dynamic companies at the right time can mean the difference between a comfortable retirement and an incredible one. It will be up to you to determine how far you can go.

To begin with, you'll need sufficient funds to be able to buy quality companies and to diversify your portfolio. I got my first lesson in diversification when I was a young carpentry subcontractor. After a few years of working for commercial builders I had put away enough money to build a rental property for myself. I saw the builders I was working for getting wealthy. I went to one of the more successful builders and told him my plans. I asked if he had any good advice for me. He told me I shouldn't consider starting until I could build ten units. A unit in his mind might be a house, an apartment, or a store. He did them all. He explained that one vacancy in a ten-unit apartment building, for instance, wasn't a big deal. One vacancy in a duplex, however, is a 50% reduction in revenue, and could prove burdensome. Oh, and the last thing he said to me was, "You know, Bill, you have done all the work and I've become a millionaire." He wasn't gloating. He was challenging me to move on and have the moxie needed to make it happen.

The same applies to investments. If you place all of your funds into one stock and that company gets in trouble, you will be jeopardizing your total investment. At this time in your investing life you should own a minimum of three companies in different industries.

If you have the moxie to begin investing and wish to dip your toe into the waters, then I would suggest doing so if you're confident you're properly prepared. When you get to that point you should be very serious about what you're doing. Use the research resources I'll suggest to make decisions about when to own certain investments and when not.

I envision the financial world as a giant virus—not a bad virus, but one that is constantly evolving. You should stay current and know how those changes are affecting your positions. This will take some effort, but not much. Once you're involved in the market you'll be surprised at how slowly these changes take place. If you're looking at the long haul, you won't have to spend all your time guarding your positions. When I use the words "long haul" I don't mean years, as many authors I've read do. When I say "long haul" I'm referring to the next six to twelve months. When I refer to "short haul" I'm talking about daily action.

Daily action leads to day trading: buying stocks and selling them several times a day on tiny profits or losses. I would advise beginners to resist being dragged into this crazy world. I haven't been able to find out what the success rate of day trading is. I think that's because it's not good. I'm sure if it were good the large investment houses that have been encouraging such action would be boasting about it.

I have a friend whose father had been a sensible person his whole life. He lost his entire life savings day trading. At 80 years of age he got caught up in the excitement of it all and put himself in jeopardy. You may think that because he was old he wasn't up to the challenge that a younger, quicker mind could handle. What if you're wrong, though? At the very time you are trying to build a foundation you could squander that start and set yourself back several years.

My advice is to stay away from day trading until you can afford losing in exchange for the excitement some people experience. I've always felt that if I wanted to lose money, I'd go to a casino. Casinos have shows, excitement, beautiful people, free drinks if you lose enough, even free rooms and dining if you really lose a lot. Day trading offers none of these enticements. Sitting in front of a computer eight hours a day is my idea of absolute boredom.

But I wander. To get back to diversification: as I mentioned earlier, my builder mentor suggested ten units to be safe. Now that may not be necessary with stocks, but the principal is the same. If you research your buys and monitor them as I'll suggest, shares in as few as three or four stocks will be okay to start with. Later on you can expand to ten good investments for more diversification. More than ten will require more time than you may be willing to devote to monitoring them correctly.

When you're attempting to diversify you'll be looking for companies in sectors that are currently "hot". A sector is a group of companies, also referred to as industries, that do the same thing. When internet and telecommunication stocks fell on their faces in 2000, other sectors stepped up to take their places. I'm told that even during our horrible depression that started in 1929, tobacco stocks did fine. Your job will be to find out which sectors are thriving. You'll buy them and sell holdings you have in faltering sectors. This will not be difficult but will require a small amount of diligence.

I know what you're thinking at this point. How can I possibly invest successfully when I have no experience or knowledge of how to do so? That is what this book is all about. When you've absorbed this book, all the imagined complexities of investing will become clearer and less daunting. You'll know where to go to receive the very best guidance and how to apply it for best results. There's no reason why a small investor cannot out perform, by far, professional money managers. If you can read, have a grip on your emotions, and apply the good principals presented in this book, you will do fine.

9

RESEARCH

When you first begin looking into the world of investing research and analysis you will probably be, as I was, overwhelmed by the number of companies and individuals eager to sell you their expert advice on how to seek your fortune. There exist thousands of experts covering everything imaginable.

Over the years I have been enticed into and down many dead end roads, and have come to the conclusion that the best way for the average beginning investor to build wealth over time is by owning high quality U.S. stocks and monitoring them carefully.

The purpose of this book is to show you how to search out and invest in the very best companies at the best time to own them. Good reliable and truthful research is hard to find, and that's why my list is so short.

When I hear someone say, "I'm going to do my own research" it sends chills up my spine. When I ask them what they mean by research the usual answers are vague, unorganized, and in my mind very scary. Many beginning investors do not realize the difficulty of research. Even if they have been exceptionally successful in every other aspect of their lives, they are not likely to do a better job than the right professional financial analysts.

Good research entails more than reading financial newspapers and magazines or watching financial TV channels. In fact, good analysis requires more than breaking down a company's financials in order to project future sales and profits.

Good analysts investigate far more than the obvious. They look at management's history, break down the company's business model, examine its governance record, determine proper timing to own the company, and a multitude of other matters.

To research the overall market in order to isolate a few superior investments requires an inordinate amount of time, experience, and know-how. Realizing that the people at *Value Line*, for example, have been doing this for over seventy years, and have developed computer models that screen millions of data items is humbling indeed. No one should think he or she can do better.

I suspect the problem today is that anyone who has been watching the markets for the past few years has begun to doubt the abilities of professional analysts because of their poor track records. This is certainly understandable when so many investors have seen their portfolios decimated since 2000.

By using the researchers I suggest you can be assured that you will be receiving the very best research. It will be free of the influence of any hidden agendas that could harm you. I'm convinced that any amateur investor who decides to do his own research is playing a very dangerous game. By knowing top-notch sources on which to base your decisions, and by using the methods presented in this book, you will be light years ahead of most other small investors.

If you're not comfortable using just the two sources I recommend, tread carefully. If you decide to use another source, be sure it is a pure research company not affiliated with a larger company. Such a relationship could have other interests that could taint the research. In the next chapter I'll discuss in more detail the research they offer.

10

WHO CAN'T BE TRUSTED?

You've seen my warnings about depending on analysis from individuals who work for large companies who may not have your best interests in mind. Yes, they will and do lie in order to profit from deceptive practices.

It may help you to understand how all of this came about by looking at a brief history of the stock market.

After the United States came out of the 1929 depression, the government called in a group of very wealthy and powerful Wall Street individuals. These men had accumulated their wealth as a direct result of the collapse of the country's financial establishment. Their ability to understand the working of the markets allowed them to gobble up the wealth of all those poor individuals who lost everything. The crash had shaken the very foundations of the American way and caused many to doubt if a free and democratic government was possible.

The individuals were appointed to a committee whose task was to outline a set of rules that would prevent another financial catastrophe like the one we had just experienced. Miraculously, they agreed to take on the task, and presented what they felt would protect individual investors in the future.

One of the primary suggestions was to set up what's known as a Chinese firewall between different entities in the financial world. For instance, a large banking firm would not be permitted to own a brokerage company. This suggestion and many others were accepted and implemented.

Unfortunately, over time these controls were slowly chipped away until the markets were ripe again for another major collapse. In other words, those powerful bankers and brokerage firms collaborated to line their pockets to the detriment of their very own clients.

Let's look at how they accomplished these dastardly deeds. Let's say a very large banking concern was courting a fledgling publicly traded company. When representatives of the bank and company meet, the bankers bring along their hotshot celebrity analyst from the brokerage company they own. At the meeting, they imply that if the publicly traded company will give the bank all of its banking business, this analyst will pump up their company in his analysis. This paints a bright future for the company and doesn't seem too bad at first glance. But what if the company that's being so highly praised stumbles, gets into trouble, or falls on its face? If the analyst continues to praise the failing company, still issuing "buys" on it just to reel in the banking business, that's where the problems arise.

During the late 1990s this very problem was rampant. You may wonder why a professional analyst would jeopardize his reputation by lying. The answer is clear. Money. Some of those charlatans were being paid mega millions to mislead the investing community. Investors were paying $200–$300 a share for companies with no earnings and no history. Brand new companies with inexperienced management were awash in money. One particular company with a twenty three year old C.E.O. received $250 million from its initial public offering.

Of course, this and many similar companies failed and the whole house of cards came tumbling down, beginning in 2000. Many of the dot coms and high tech companies stock prices fell precipitously, some into oblivion.

Amazingly, all during these horrific times many brokerage firms and analysts were still issuing "buy" recommendations to their clients. And even more incredibly, many of those same analysts are still around shopping their wares. Still advising a whole new generation of investors.

What I'm doing here is showing you why you should be so careful when doing research on companies, and why my suggested sources are so few. Diversity in this case is not a good idea. My two primary sources, *Value Line* and *Investor's Business Daily*, I trust totally to give me accurate and truthful analysis. They aren't always right, no one is, but you can be assured their work is honest.

11

DOING YOUR HOMEWORK

When novices begin investing, many if not most can become overwhelmed by the amount of technical information available. Web sites, magazines, newspapers, financial books are everywhere. Can any of these be trusted to give honest and accurate guidance? I struggled for many years reading every magazine and book I could get my hands on, only to become more and more confused. Eventually I came upon the sources I suggest any new investor search out and follow.

First I suggest going to your local library and digesting *The Value Line*. You don't need the information in a particular issue, but how to use the publication. The analysts at *Value Line* are not influenced by pressures that could alter their evaluation of the companies they are covering. I've devoted a chapter to this publication; I consider it to be the prime source for guidance for all investors.

Besides *Value Line* I highly recommend *Investor's Business Daily (IBD)*. *IBD* is a daily financial newspaper. Founded by William J. O'Neil, *IBD* not only reports on the market, but works very hard to educate the general public about how to invest properly. You'll find *IBD* at most libraries or newsstands. Subscriptions are currently $295 per year.

Value Line is where I begin looking for a superior investment, and then I go to *IBD* to refine that research. Whereas *Value Line* uses proprietary methods to value stocks, *IBD* not only looks at each stock's underlying strengths, it also looks at how the market is treating those stocks and shows how they do their analysis. For instance, *IBD* teaches that large moves in stock prices are caused by large institutional investors (currently 70–75% of all investment volume)

34

bidding those stocks up or down. Knowing what those large institutional investors are up to can be an enormous help to you. *IBD* shows how to gain and use this information. Institutional investing is only one of seven tools used to measure a stock's strength and future prospects by *IBD*. The seven tools are listed in the CANSLIM toolbox, where each letter represents a different measure to help identify future winners.

> C = Current Quarterly Earnings
> A = Annual Earnings Increases
> N = NEW products, NEW management, NEW highs
> S = Supply and Demand—Shares outstanding plus big volume demand
> L = Leader or Laggard
> I = Institutional Sponsorship
> M = Market Direction

By using CANSLIM you're searching out, not good companies to invest with, but the very best companies in the most dynamic sectors; companies with excellent business models and management at the proper time in the business cycle to allow them to excel in the next six to twelve months.

One more thing I might mention about *IBD*. If you absolutely do not have the time to study all of this or if the whole minutiae of choosing good investments bores you to tears there is an easy way out. With a subscription to *IBD* you gain access to *IBD*'s website investor.com free of additional charge. On this website, each company has been rated from A (best) to E using CAN SLIM. Using these ratings, you can reduce your list of 100 companies from *Value Line* down to a smaller number of A-rated companies. Now you have a short list of companies who show the most promise to charge ahead and are also being gobbled up by the large institutions. When that happens, they all jump on, driving prices beyond what is true value for the stock. At this point, you have joined in and are riding the wave up with them.

Adversely, those very same larger institutional buyers can and do drop those very stocks when they see the upper momentum stalling. They all watch each other and follow along. The selling results in a nosedive in the price of that particular stock. Now the stock will continue falling over time as more investors are frightened out of their positions.

Unfortunately, many small investors are standing there wanting to know from their broker what is happening. The broker will then come up with some cockamamie story of why and suggest getting out of the position and getting into something better. "Hurrah," the broker thinks, "I just made two commissions." And that can explain why the stock of apparently good companies with no bad news can suddenly plummet for no apparent reason.

These events can be so severe that a company's share price can fall far below its fair market value. At this point, guess who's ready to gobble up huge chunks of that poor downtrodden company? Certainly not the small investors. They were burned once; it's not going to happen to them again. Yes, the institutional buyers again, and the cycle begins anew.

It's very important to be aware of what's happening with your positions. Homework doesn't end when you buy a stock. If you have placed your stop loss under the price of your position, as I suggest in Chapter 14, a sudden drop in price won't seriously harm you. By learning how to interpret volume, you will know what's happening as it's happening. You will then know when to exit your position.

To interpret volume may seem complicated, but it's not. Basically, when a price is rising on huge volume the big boys are involved. When the price continues rising on low volume the poor latecomers (small investors) are continuing to bid the price up. When the price begins to fall on large volume, the big boys are dumping their positions. Basically that's how you use volume to save your skin. Your stop order will bump you out as the stock falls.

There's one more place I check to refine my list of potential buys. *IBD* has a list of sectors, 197 in all. A <u>sector</u> is a group of companies that do the same kind of work. The reason I like *IBD*'s sectors best is because they break down the sectors into smaller parts. For instance, another list might list computers as one sector, while *IBD* will break that sector into computer manufacturers, software producers, etc. One part of a sector may be sailing while another part could be slowing.

This list is important because even during a recession some sectors do well. For instance, during our latest recession telecom and internet sectors fell on their faces. Yet housing, precious metals and auto stocks have done fine. By staying abreast of which sectors are losing steam and which ones are moving up to take their places, you can adjust your portfolio to protect your profits.

After you have reduced your *Value Line* top 100 equities down to a lesser number by selecting those companies that are found in the best performing sectors, move on to *Investor's Business Daily* to further whittle down the list. Find which companies on your short list that have an "A" rating there.Any one of them would probably be an excellent buy. Instead of blindfolding yourself and pointing at one, there's another place to go. *Standard and Poor's* (a publication also found in most libraries) lists the companies that pay strong dividends. Dividends will not always help a stock price to go up, but it's an indicator the company has their shareholders in mind.

Some would argue that companies that do not pay dividends can take their revenues and plow them back into the company, thus making the company stronger and more valuable. My experience has shown me that's not what always happens. Many companies will be tempted to waste those revenues or design huge benefit packages for management. If I'm deciding which of two companies to choose, and both are rated the same, I choose the one that has a strong dividend paying history.

Most investment books you'll read will tell you that the average gains in the market have been, over time, 10% per year. What you won't read is that almost half of those gains have been from dividends (4.5%). Today companies are not paying dividends as they have in the past (1% on average). Studies have shown that companies that pay dividends return to the investors more than companies that don't.

Imagine, of the approximately 10,000 companies available, you have reduced that number down to four or five companies. These four or five have been chosen by some of the best analysts in the world, with no vested interests to taint their work, to be the ones that will perform best in the next twelve months. You've done the work, so now you can place your order.

12

VALUE LINE

The *Value Line* system is where I begin my search for a strong company with excellent prospects for future growth. *Value* Line is an excellent analytical service that can be found in most libraries or ordered by subscription.

Each week *Value Line* ranks 1,700 stocks, comparing them to each other for timeliness.[1] Each of the 1,700 stocks are given a number rating from 1 to 5, with a number 1 being the highest, or best. Of the 1,700

    100 will be rated as 1
    300 will be rated as 2
    900 will be rated as 3
    300 will be rated as 4
    100 will be rated as 5

By selecting all number one ranked stocks to proceed with for further research, you will be lessening the field of over 10,000 equities available.

You may wonder how to choose the best of these one hundred stocks to purchase. There are many ways to make a choice, but this is the way I proceed. I touched briefly on this earlier, but it needs repeating in more detail. First, I look for the list where 98 industries are ranked for probable performance in the coming twelve months. This list is found at the bottom of the first page of the "Summary and Index Part 1". This list of industries is arranged alphabeti-

---

1. Timeliness indicates how well *Value Line's* analysts believe a particular stock will perform in the next six to twelve months.

cally. To the right of each industry name you'll find its ranking showing how it's expected to perform in relation to the others, with number one being the best. To the right of the number you'll see a page number where that particular industry is discussed.[2] On the pages following the general discussion of the industry will be analysts' reports of the individual companies in that industry that are covered by *Value Line.* By retrieving the timeliness, technical, and safety rankings from the analysts' reports you will be able to isolate the best company in that industry.

For instance, on page 867 of Issue 6, April 12, 2002 the number one ranked industry, homebuilding, is discussed. The analyst presents an overall look at the homebuilders and the reasons they should do well in the next twelve months. On the following pages, (868–881) are listed each of the fourteen companies that are part of the homebuilding industry covered by *Value Line.* Each company is ranked for timeliness, safety, and technical. I usually go through the list looking for number one rankings in timeliness and technical. In this issue only NVR meets this criterion.

Safety ratings can be lower. NVR is ranked number 3 in safety, which is okay. This doesn't mean that NVR is on shaky ground, but it is an indicator that the company's share price could be more volatile than companies rated number 1 or 2. All the companies listed here are large solid companies and a number 3 ranking should not be a problem. In fact, it could be an advantage. Volatile companies can be explosive on the upside. As long as you watch your position carefully, placing stops when needed as explained in Chapter 14, these stocks can be fun to own and potentially very profitable.

The technical rankings are *Value Line's* prediction of each stock's price performance relative to the overall market in the following three to six months. This is similar to the timeliness ranking, but over a shorter time span.

If you plan to buy more than one stock, or if you don't find one you like in the way I've described, simply go down the industry list until you find one that meets the requirements.

One more thought. If you are adding to your portfolio, diversify by selecting stocks in different industries.

The reason I remain so committed to *Value Line* is because of its incredible past record. Some would argue that past performance has nothing to do with

---

2.   These page numbers refer to Part 3 of "Ratings and Reports.

what will happen in the future. I contend that anyone who has been right for over forty years is someone I'd put my trust in.

For instance, if you started investing using *Value Line's* system in 1965, buying only number 1 rated stocks, and only rebalanced your portfolio once a year, by 2000 your investment would have increased by almost 16,000 percent, beating the Dow Industrial Average by fifteen to one.

Although those results are quite extraordinary, those figures reflect results if you only changed your positions once a year. If you updated every time one of your stocks was downgraded from a 1 to a 2, every three or four months on average, and you replaced that stock with a new stock ranked number 1, the results would be dramatically higher. *Value Line's* past results show that revising your portfolio in this way would have resulted in an astounding increase of more than 58,848 percent.

In thirty-five years, a $10,000 investment using the *Value Line* system with annual updates could be worth over $1,500,000. With updates on a more frequent basis, as individual stocks ratings rise and fall, that same $10,000 startup turns out to be worth over $6,000,000.

Remember, these numbers are the result of starting with $10,000 and never adding to your account or taking anything out of it. Suppose you kept adding funds each year. Your results would be limited only by how much you invested and how well you managed your account.

When reading this you may say to yourself, "I'm just beginning in life. Where am I going to get $10,000? I've got so many expenses I can't afford to invest." I know the feeling. One thousand dollars a year, however, comes to only $20 a week. By skimping a little each week you could fund an account that could grow to undreamed-of numbers.

Many books and articles have been written on how to save money. They suggest: driving an older car; taking your lunch to work; eating out less; stopping smoking; car-pooling; getting a second job. The men who used to work for my father said they didn't mind working on Saturdays. They said it wasn't the extra money they made as much as the money they didn't spend when off. I'm sure if you think about it you can come up with a way to get started.

That $1,000 investment will not turn into 1.6 million dollars, but $160,000 is a tidy sum considering that only 20% of Americans have saved $100,000. Let's suppose, though, you continued funding your account; rather than stopping with your first $1,000, instead adding a similar amount each year over your entire working life. That shouldn't be so difficult as you become more established in life. That small $20 per week, saved and properly managed, could grow in value enough to place your worth in the top 1% of all Americans when you're ready to retire. That is pretty incredible when you think about it. For the price of a cappuccino each day you could fund a beautiful future.

13

GOVERNANCE

"Never confuse a bull market with genius"

A large Wall Street company recently graded the one hundred largest companies on the U.S. market for good governance. They were graded from one to ten with one being poor and ten being best. Of all one hundred companies, only three received a grade of ten. That is worrisome and should be a warning to all investors.

When you're searching for a superior equity and have reduced your choices to five or ten candidates, governance could point to the best one to trust with your hard earned money. A company may be growing impressively; however, if management is spending a disproportionate amount of time on building their own wealth through outrageous pay and retirement packages rather than building the company's and investors' wealth it is basically wasting everyone's time except their own.

Speaking of outrageous behavior: during the roaring nineties when no one was watching, there actually existed consulting firms whose specialty was directing management toward the best way to legally extract the most money from a company without the fear of winding up in jail. Guess who paid those consultants? You bet, the companies. During those crazy years, when share prices were going straight up, no one was paying attention to what was happening to companies internally. Some investors were convinced that management actually deserved those outrageous salaries.

After all, when you're buying an equity for single digits and in two or three years the price zooms to $200 or $300 a share, it's only natural to assume that management are all geniuses. In 2000, however, the bubble burst. Investors, after losing a big chunk of their savings, realized that those guys were simply riding a hard driven, senseless, speculative wave that was baseless.

All the while, during those heady days, many companies' managements were furiously milking their cash cows for all they were worth, arguing that they deserved it. "After all, we're making you rich, why shouldn't you pay us well for that?" I think many of them actually believed it.

Since then, the investment world has awakened. Many companies are now hiring CGOs, or corporate governance officers, to basically protect the owners of the company (investors) from greedy management. This should be the job of the board of directors, but as long as the CEO (Chief Executive Officer) recommends to shareholders the directors, there exists an obvious conflict of interest. CGOs may help, but as long as they report to the CEOs there is still plenty of room for future hanky panky.

When isolating the very best company to invest with, governance can be the deciding factor for identifying a future star. Fortunately, there are services that grade companies for good governance. These include GovernanceMetrics, Institutional Shareholders Services Inc., and recently Morningstar.

GovernanceMetrics analyzes 600 data points, rating companies from 1 (best) on down.

Knowing how a company is treating their shareholders will help you immensely. Michael Douglas told us in the movie *Wall Street* that greed is good. I would agree, but not outrageous greed. Compensating management for a job well done is an excellent motivator, but to a point.

As we have seen in the past few years, management can run amok, bringing giant companies to their knees and affecting hundreds of thousands of individuals. Lost jobs, lost savings, and shattered retirement plans are the obvious results, but what about the world's conception of the American way of doing business? If we can't teach business ethics and then have the intelligence to monitor results and prosecute wrongdoers, we will all be in trouble. After all, who in the world would invest in a system where poor governance is rampant? This is some gloomy stuff, but you need to be cognizant of the darker side. I would not be doing my job if I only painted the pretty side of what you're taking on.

Now let's summarize the process when searching out a prime candidate to own:

1. Find the number one ranked companies from *Value Line*

2. Of those 100 companies, isolate the ones that are in the best performing sectors

3. With that list, go to *IBD* and find which ones are rated "A"

4. If more than one remains, see which has the best rating as far as governance (*Morningstar)* and dividend paying history (your broker).

14

SMALL & MID CAP SURVEY

In 1996 *Value Line* began a new service that covers 1,800 small and mid-cap stocks not included in their standard service. This new service costs $510 per year and may not be available at your library. Don't worry about the cost though, because, as you might expect, I've come up with a way to save on this cost until you can afford to purchase your own. More about that in Chapter 19.

Many would advise beginners to stay clear of small or mid-caps because of their small funding, lack of management history, and track record. All true, if an investor was only guessing or buying on hearsay. *Value Line*, however, takes each of the 1,800 stocks included in this service and breaks them down the same way they do the larger companies in their standard edition of large cap stocks. They place a numerical value from one to five on each stock for performance, technical, and safety.

I suggest that beginners consider investing a portion of their funds, perhaps 10%, in small or mid-cap equities because of the profit history of the *Value Line* survey. Since its inception in 1996 their results have been phenomenal. During that short timeframe their #1 ranked stocks have averaged **128% per year increase**, or 1,026.1% total in the eight years from 1996 to 2004. In case that percentage didn't sink in, try multiplying $1,000 times 128% ten times. Could I be wrong, or is this $3,796,194.67?

I'm not suggesting that a small investor can expect such phenomenal results. When using averages, unless you own all of the stock, there's no guarantee you will buy the best performers. By definition, half of the group will be above average and the rest will be below. However, if you do the same due diligence as you do when choosing larger companies you'll have a good chance of owning the better performers. You won't have as much history to work with, but by selecting companies from the best performing sectors, you'll have a leg up. So that's why I suggest using a piece of your funds for small and mid-cap companies.

Here's how to do it: Look up the *Value Line Small and Mid Cap Survey* model portfolio located in the "Summary Index." The stocks listed in the model portfolio are the companies they have selected to have above average price potential in the coming year.

Right now I'm looking at the January 9, 2004 edition. I look at the model portfolio for that week and scan down both the performance and the technical rank columns to find out which companies have a #1 ranking for both. On this day, there are only four.

The next column ranks each company for safety. Here we're not looking for a #1 ranking, as strange as this may seem. Companies with #1 safety ratings, as mentioned earlier, do not possess the explosive price increase potentials as do, say, #3s.

On this day, just one company combines #1 ratings in both performance and technical rank columns with a #3 in safety. That is the company I will invest in today. If there should be more than one candidate, check to see which one is in the best performing sector and buy it. It's that easy.

You should continue holding that stock until it's bumped off the model portfolio. At that time, replace it with another using the same method.

You may feel this whole thing is just too cavalier for your liking. What's important here is not how much work you have put into these decisions, but how much total work has been put into them. Just remember that some of the best analysts in the world have done all the digging for you, and have presented their conclusions to you in a truthful manner with no hidden agendas. Then you won't feel guilty about not working so hard at investing.

If this method intrigues you but you're not totally convinced you should trust *Value Line*, why not contact them and ask for their promotional literature for both their standard and small and mid-cap surveys. I think you'll agree with me: there's no better source to help you make your decisions.

15

HOW TO BUY A STOCK

You have now set up your trading account with the brokerage firm of your choice. After due diligence you have chosen a company to buy shares of stock. You should have your account number in front of you along with the name of the company you wish to buy, its ticker symbol, the number of shares you wish to buy, the price per share, and the type of order, which we will discuss in a minute.

In order to have a record of my trading activity, I like to list this order in my daybook in the following way:

Date
Time of day
Name of company
Ticker symbol
Bid/Ask Prices
Type of Order (Buy or Sell Short)
Market/Limit and limit price
Fill date
Fill price
Proof (Confirmation number)
Stop-loss price

If you're not online and must deal with a broker, first identify yourself to your broker by name and account number. Next ask what the bid and ask price is for the company you're interested in. Write the two numbers on your sheet. Next, if you are buying long, place your order at a slightly higher price than the bid price. This is known as a LIMIT order. The reason for doing so is, usually if you just place a market order without stipulating a price your broker will buy it as quickly as possible *but with no price guarantee.* This may seem insignificant, but over time it is important. Many times you can save much more than the commission with this simple technique.

If your order cannot be filled immediately while you're on the phone, ask that you be notified when it is filled. Most of the time you'll get your price, but it may take a little longer. If by the next day you have not received the fill call, inquire into the status of your order. Sometimes your broker will forget to call you back. I have even had them forget to place an order. By law, they are not responsible for such mistakes, you are. Going online makes everything much easier and simpler. By pulling up your account page you'll be able to click on "open orders" and within seconds verify your records. I do so every day. Keep on top of things. Keep good records

If the broker was not able to fill the order, you may need to raise your offer and try again. Oftentimes a buyer or seller will come up or down to your offer. Be sure that when you make your new offer that the old "good until cancelled" order is cancelled. If it is not, you could wind up buying or selling a stock sometime in the future when you don't want to. If your broker is on the ball this will not happen, but they aren't always so. This may seem trivial, but I once saw an investor financially ruined by not abiding by this seemingly obvious rule. In fact, if you are not checking online, you should call your broker periodically to be sure you have no outstanding orders active that you may have forgotten. Better yet, keep excellent records and call your broker to verify those records. Just ask, "Do I have any open orders?"

16

WHEN TO SELL A STOCK

"When there are no fish in one spot, cast your net in another"

—Chinese proverb

To this point we've discussed how to use *Value Line* and *Investor's Business Daily* to select excellent companies poised to increase in value. We also talked about selling a company when *Value Line* downgrades it from a #1 ranking. You may not feel comfortable waiting around for *Value Line's* moves. For that reason I'd like to discuss trailing stop losses.

First let's look at using the "Standard *Value Line* Survey." Because it surveys large cap stocks your stop losses can be placed closer than if you owned small or mid-cap stocks. Small and mid-cap stocks tend to be more volatile than their big brothers and stop orders must be placed further away (25%) to avoid being bumped out prematurely.

Because none of us can see into the future some simple rules must be adopted to take the guesswork out of decisions regarding when to sell a stock. Always remember you're not marrying a stock; just borrowing it until the picture changes.

A simple procedure used at the time you purchase a stock will automatically cut your losses. Place what is called a stop loss, (simply a sell order at a stipulated price, good until canceled), at 8% below your purchase price if you're buying long, reversed if you're selling short. This way, if you were wrong and your stock takes a nosedive, your losses would be minimized. Not a good thing to happen, but one you will experience occasionally. This way your funds and spirit will not be damaged too much.

Stop losses may be one of the hardest rules to follow. When you buy a particular stock you have invested considerable time and effort selecting it, and it's only natural to want to stay with the choices you've made. Instead you may reason that you'll give them a little more downside. Surely they will turn around. But if the price continues falling, and by then you've sustained a considerable loss, you may reason that the price can't possibly go any lower. I'm sure that when the tech bubble burst in 2000, a lot of that type of thinking was going on. However, over the next two years, many of those high flying stocks fell 90% in value, and some 100%. In depth studies by *IBD* and others show that using stop losses, over time, is the best way to preserve capital.

Here's an example of how stop losses, if used correctly, will protect you if you purchase a stock based on faulty information.

On June 22, 2001, after giving a glowing picture of a company's past performance and present conditions, a stock analyst concluded with the following synopsis for the future of this particular company: "This neutrally ranked issue has solid 3–5 year appreciation prospects." The analyst was Todd A. Schwartzman and at that time he worked for *Value Line*. The company he was reporting on was Enron Corporation, which turned out to be one of the largest failures in U.S. business history. Huge investor losses occurred shortly after the above report.

I didn't choose this incident to deride *Value Line* or Mr. Schwartzman, but to emphasize how important stop losses are for protecting your nest egg. Good analysis is based on information believed to be true. If a company misrepresents itself, then good analysis is not possible on that company. So, therefore, stop losses protect us if such misrepresentations occur. As Forrest Gump reminded us, "stuff happens."

Stop losses help not only if we make bad choices, they also help if something bad happens to a good company when we own it. This could be something under the company's control, such as a management mistake, or something outside its control, such as a competitor developing a better product or service.

When this happens to a company, small investors like you may not hear about it until the share price has dropped considerably. At some time in your investment life something of this nature will happen to a company you own a piece of. If it's as dramatic as what happened at Enron, your finances could be seriously damaged. Don't be lazy. Use stop losses—they're free insurance.

Now let's get back to the proper use of stop losses. We'll assume that you were correct and the share price of the stock you purchased begins to rise. The conventional procedure is to cancel the old stop loss and place a new one 8% below the current price, and continue doing so as the price continues higher. This is known as a trailing stop loss.

Investor's Business Daily suggests a better way to protect your positions. They reason that because no stock goes up in a straight line, you would probably be knocked out of your position somewhere along its rise in price if you continued placing the trailing stop loss at 8% below the current price. Therefore, you would never participate in a gigantic price rise of a company. Instead of maintaining a trailing stop loss, you would decide when to exit your positions depending on your ability to interpret the market action and volume.

Here's how I suggest using stop losses. When you enter a position place a stop loss 8% below your entry price. When the price reaches 10% above your entry price, cancel your existing stop loss and place a new stop loss at your entry price, including commissions. At that time, you have locked in a virtual no-loss position.

Then, instead of following behind with new stop losses as the stock progresses higher, you leave your break-even stop loss in place. Continue to monitor your position to determine when to exit. You will do this online using the charts provided by your brokerage house or *Value Line*. When the price of your stock drops below its fifty day moving average at the same time that the volume climbs above its fifty day average you're being told that the big institutions are exiting from their positions and you should, too.

By knowing that most large movements in stock prices, either up or down, are caused by large institutional buying or selling, you will know when to sell your position. And, you may ask, how will you know that, and what is a fifty day moving average on large volume?

Okay, a fifty day moving average is represented by the solid line on the following chart that tells you, at any particular time, what the average price for that stock has been over the past fifty days. It will help you determine when a stock's upward movement has slowed and is possibly ready to fall. At the bottom of the chart a bar graph shows the volume of stock bought and sold for the same time period.

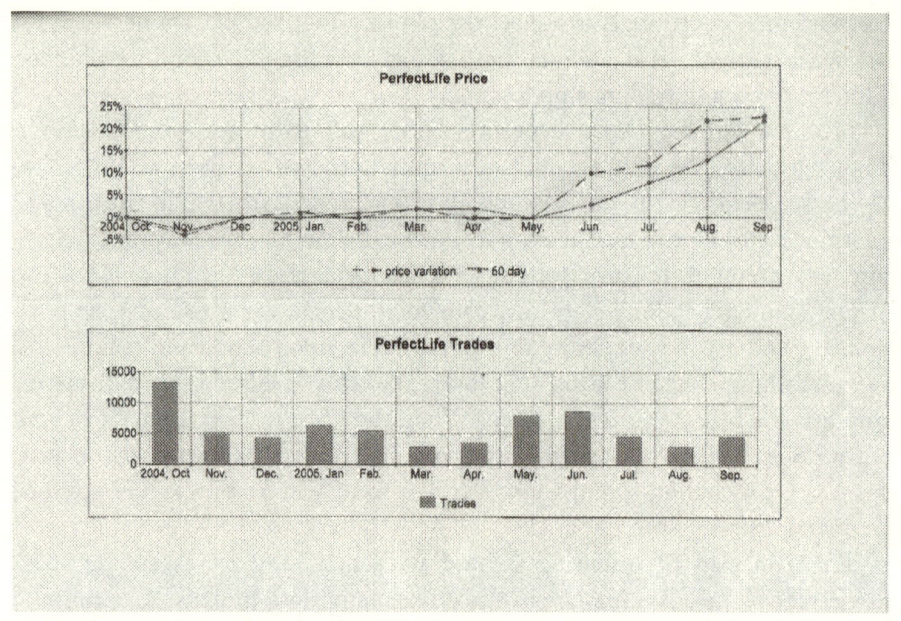

Of course, you can't be positive the price won't turn around again and continue rising. For that reason, I don't sell right then. Instead, I first cancel my break-even stop loss and place a new stop loss 8% below the price where it penetrated the fifty day moving average.

In that way, if the price turns around and continues in its upward move, I'll still own it. I can continue monitoring my position until it drops back below its fifty day moving average again. I continue this procedure until I am eventually stopped out, but during that time I have ridden along as far as I safely could.

Using this method will allow you to own a stock as long as it is making you profits and will get you out when the price turns down.

That's how to use stop losses properly if you own large caps. As mentioned earlier, if you're involved with small caps I'd suggest using a 25% stop loss because of the excessive volatility they experience.

The following chart will help explain how stop losses applied correctly will tell you when to exit your position.

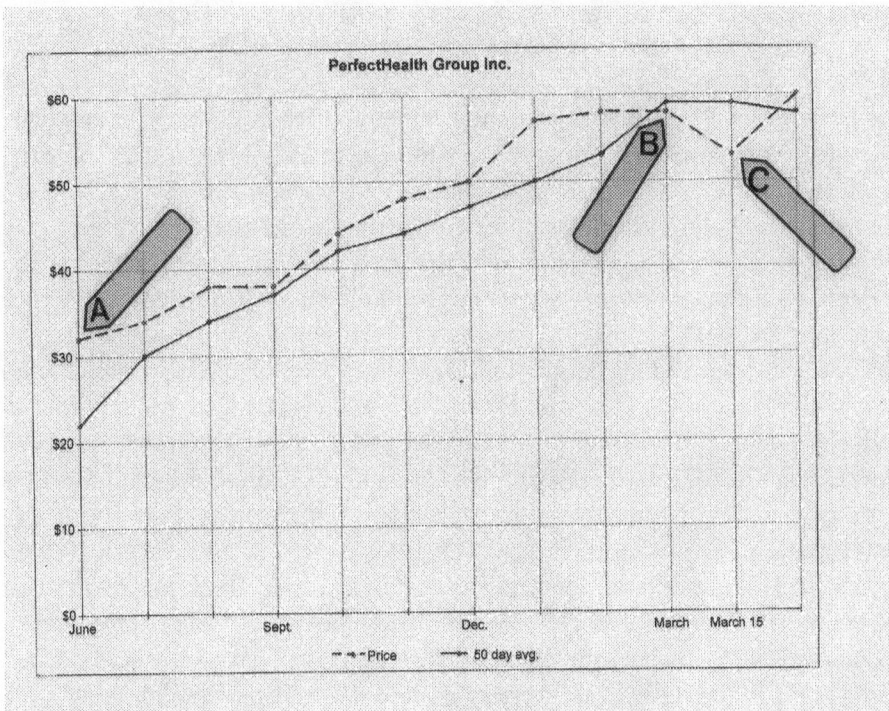

Let's say you bought a long position in PerfectHealth Group Inc. in June of 2000 when all your indicators said you should (A). Your entry price was $32 and you placed a stop loss 8% below your entry. As suggested, you cancelled your original stop loss and placed a new one at break even when the price increased to 10% above your cost.

You then only needed to monitor your position until March when the price dropped below its 50 day moving average (B) at $58. You then cancelled your break even stop loss and placed a new one at $53.36 (58 * .08 = 4.64; 58—4.64 = 53.36). Two weeks later, you were stopped out (C). Your profit on the position would have been $21.36 per share minus commissions. A nice 66.75% profit in nine and a half months (21.36/32 = .6675 = 66.75%)

It is impossible to over-emphasize the importance of canceling an existing stop loss order when placing a new one. This is because it is possible to sell stock you do not own. This is called "selling short" and when you do it, you are then obliged to purchase the stock that you sold. If the price continues to fall, and you buy at a

*lower price, you're in luck and made money on the deal. But it is a tricky thing to
do at best, and very dangerous when done unintentionally.*

Let's set up a hypothetical situation to help clarify this important and dangerous part of investing. Suppose we had bought 100 shares of the company discussed above. We bought at $32/share and placed a stop loss at $29.44. Now, just as before, the share price rose, dropped down below the fifty day moving average at $58. At that time you placed a new stop loss at $53.36. The price then dropped down to your stop loss and you were stopped out of your position. But let's suppose that when you were placing your new stop at $53.36 you forgot to cancel the old break-even stop loss. That original stop loss will no longer be protection for you, but will instead turn into an order to sell short shares you thought were behind you. If the price then drops down low enough to trigger your short sell order, and then turns around and begins rising, you could be losing considerable funds without even knowing it was happening.

As you might expect, there are exceptions to the preceding method of deciding when to sell a stock. There will be times when the price of a stock you own will enter what's known as a blow-off stage. This usually occurs when professionals and individual investors go into a "feeding frenzy", bidding up a stock's price far beyond its true value.

If this happens to a stock you own, great!, but be realistic and realize you should be more on your guard than ever. When these blow-offs occur they can and do fall from grace fast and far. By knowing the signs of a blow-off you can get out of your position before it penetrates its 50 day moving average. The chart on the next page is a prime example of when you should take your profits.

So what are some of the warning signs that tell us a stock is approaching its peak and you should exit? If a stock you own is moving up nicely for several months and suddenly begins an upward move disproportionate to its normal weekly price moves, its probably entering into a blow-off phase. This is especially true if the stock's price begins to open higher than it closed the night before (known as an exhaustion gap).

It may help if you know what's happening about this time to cause all of this craziness. Not only are average investors clamoring to buy this stock they probably wouldn't have bought just weeks earlier for half the price, but professionals are, in a strange way, driving the price higher. The professional investors know when a stock is excessively priced. When they think the price has topped out, they begin to short the stock (selling stock they do not own), and placing a stop loss (a buy order) *above* their entering position. Now because everything is so chaotic, and more investors are bidding the price higher, the stop loss price of the shorters is reached. They must buy those stocks they shorted, at a loss, thus driving the price even higher. This can happen again and again over several days before the price finally peaks, stalls, and begins to fall. While this is occurring, the institutions are selling to the small investors (lemmings). When the fall begins, the institutions bail out, the shorters are riding down with glee, the small investors panic-sell at a loss, and prices continue down.

When you own a stock and you recognize a blow-off occurring, don't think about waiting for the price to drop back to the 50 day moving average. As you can see from the following chart, it was wise to get out during the last throes of the blow-off phase.

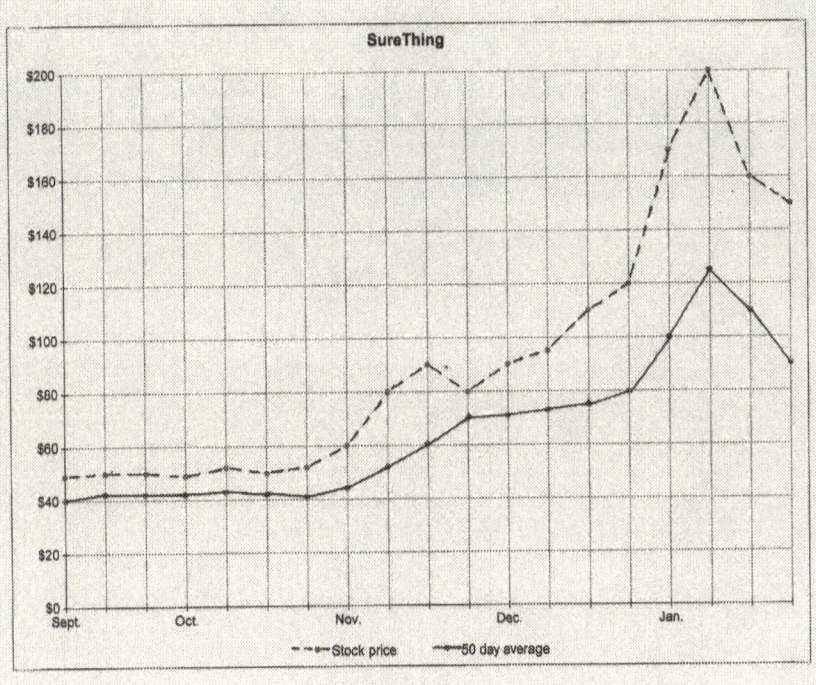

By the way, the charts in this chapter are greatly simplified to avoid confusion and to illustrate the points I'm making. The charts you'll see online or in *IBD* and *Value Line* are much more detailed, often showing daily changes. With experience, you'll be able to understand and interpret their complexities.

17

KEEPING GOOD RECORDS

"'The horror of that moment,' the King went on, 'I shall never, never forget.'
'You will, though,' the Queen said, 'if you don't make a memorandum of it.'"

—Lewis Carroll in *Through the Looking Glass.*

Keeping good records of all your trades as they occur is important. Doing so will enable you to have quick reference to what you paid for each equity, what your costs were (commissions, fees), what your selling price was, your profit/loss and when these occurred.

You can make up a chart in a notebook or on a computer spreadsheet (see the illustration at the end of this chapter). List each buy in chronological order and leave a row open between each to fill in the sell information. When you sell the stock, fill it in and calculate your profit/loss numbers.

It's a good idea to develop good habits such as this in the beginning. Later on, as you become more active these good records will make your trading life less stressful and help to eliminate costly mistakes.

Good records are essential at tax time, making it easy to determine if turn-around (time between buy and sell) was a long- or short-term capital gain and the tax due. If your account is tax-deferred or sheltered this info will not matter to the IRS. However, your accountant will still want that information, because that's the way accountants are. Anyway good record-keeping is important if for no other reason than to let you know how you're doing.

Another good habit I suggest is to have, in addition to your profit/loss record, a transaction log. Note in your log every transaction you make, with proof. When you place an order online you'll receive a confirmation number confirming that your order has been received and is being processed. If you place an order to a broker, he won't give you that number. That is why all verbal orders are audio recorded. Recordings protect your broker and you in the event of a misunderstanding. Jot down any confirmation numbers in your transaction log and transfer them to your permanent record when convenient.

I once read that ten experts were asked to look over the investment histories of 25 volunteer investors. The experts were looking for problems and making suggestions for improvement. In all but two cases, every expert mentioned "keeps poor records". When confronted with this particular problem, each investor admitted to being lazy in this respect. They said they had, in the past, sometimes become confused and had lost money because of their poor record keeping.

If you don't know where you are you can't possibly know which way to go.

This may seem trivial, but believe me, meticulous records are important. People make mistakes. Being able to solve disputes quickly is important and keeping good complete records will definitely help.

Date	Buy/Sell	Proof	Symbol	Quantity	Price	Fee/ Commission	Cost/ Total Sell Price	Profit/ Loss
1/21/ 2003	Bought	888	XYZ	100	$3.58	+10	$368.00	
3/16/ 2003	Sold	888	XYZ	100	$5.00	-10	$490.00	$122.00

18

INVESTMENT CLUBS

I have not been keen on investment clubs in the past, feeling that the disadvantages outweigh the positive aspects by a large margin. Investment clubs seem to me another opportunity for extroverts to socialize, get some investment tips, and eat cookies. I never wanted to jeopardize my financial future investing by committee.

However, if you think you would enjoy being a part of a conventional investment club, you might think about forming one with friends or family. In Julie Stav's book *Getting Your Share* (Berkley Books, New York, 2000) she devotes a chapter to starting an investment club. She explains where to get the help you need, and some of the problems you may encounter. If you can't find her book in your local library try contacting her online, where she has generously offered her help to investors looking to set up a club. The web site is http://www.juliestav.com.

I suggest that investment clubs can play a part in your investment life, but not in the conventional way. If, for instance, you live in a place where good, reliable research material is not available free (from public or academic libraries), the costs could be burdensome, especially for beginners. By gathering together a group of like-minded individuals, those costs could be shared while eliminating the negative aspects of conventional investment clubs. Meeting weekly, the group members could read the recent reports, discuss them, make their own decisions, and invest as they see fit using their own brokerage account. That should appeal to investors who are tax-sheltered in an IRA.

The *Value Line Small and Mid-Cap Survey* costs $10 a week. Suppose a small group of ten investors met and discussed the latest report. The cost of this outstanding research source per member would be just $1 a week. This may appear to be penny pinching, but try to keep in mind when making decisions such as this—a dollar saved and invested can enrich your future life tremendously over time. Besides, you might meet some nice people along the way.

Some of the other advantages offered by this type of investment club are

- No need to register with the IRS

- Each person will invest his/her own funds using an individual account

- Elimination of arguments and bickering over investment decisions

- No takeover by pushy individuals

- No bookkeeping necessary

I suggest not having dues as it places a burden on one person to keep the books, hassle people to pay up, and find a place to keep the money. Instead, let the members decide which research resources they wish the club to subscribe to, divide the total amount by the number of members with each member paying once a year. You will still need to have a designated subscriber for each or all resources. If a member drops out they lose the rest of the year unless they can find someone to buy the remainder of the year from them. (Most investment clubs have waiting lists of eager prospective members.) If someone doesn't show up for a meeting, that's their loss. Sounds picky, but setting up bylaws in advance can help to avoid squabbles later on. After all, the whole idea of investment clubs is to help every member prosper. A pleasant environment makes it even better. Julie Stav says that many investment clubs break up because of petty bickering and unpleasantness.

19

WHERE WE'VE BEEN:
A SUMMARY

The following outline summarizes the proper sequence of moves for a successful investing life. This assumes that you do not have an opportunity to place your savings in a company 401(k).

a. Develop a saving habit no matter how small, as early in life as possible.

b. Open an online brokerage account.

c. Sign up for an individual retirement (IRA) account through your broker.

d. Begin funding your IRA and instruct your broker to place those funds in a money market fund.

e. When your account has accumulated sufficient funds, buy into a total market index fund.

f. If you are not computer literate, begin taking courses to become so.

g. Visit your local library to learn how to use *Value Line Survey* and *Investor's Business Daily* or subscribe to these publications.

h. When you're confident you understand how to use *Value Line* and *IBD*, begin searching out and buying individual stocks as described in this book.

i.   As your funds allow, continue to add more stocks until retirement.

j.   Carefully monitor the stocks you own in the time-tested fashion presented here.

k.   Enjoy an incredible retirement!

20

ADVANCED LEARNING

"When we accept tough jobs as a challenge and wade into them with joy and enthusiasm, miracles can happen."

—Harry Truman, 33rd U.S. President.

Up to now we have discussed how to use *IBD* and both the *Value Line* Standard and Small and Mid-Cap publications. I'm confident that a beginning investor, with little effort or knowledge, using these three publications as I've suggested, will make a success of investing. By trusting the people at *Value Line* and *IBD* to guide you and by using the few rules presented in this book to protect yourself, I'm sure your future financial life will be better than most. No further study is necessary.

However, if you're not satisfied with this and want to learn more, I would suggest reading the books and articles listed in the bibliography.

Be very suspicious when others make outrageous claims. Just ask yourself this: "If their claims are true, why is it that almost all of the most knowledgeable individuals in the investment world seldom beat the market averages?"

What I have tried to do with this book is show small investors how to find trustworthy, reliable sources to guide them with their choices and how to protect themselves from forces that could ruin them. Any other attempts to fine tune what I've suggested could be confusing and dangerous for beginners.

21

SOME FINAL WORDS

"When you arrive at your future, will you blame your past?"

—Robert Half, entrepreneur

I'm sure many "experts" will consider this little book to be an over-simplification of a very complex and complicated universe. I would argue that the market is only complicated if you allow it to be. Let's look at where we've been.

We discussed how many of the strategies bandied about are too complex and dangerous for beginners.

We've discovered how most individuals are easily manipulated and sold a bill of goods that benefits mostly those selling them.

We've talked about who you can trust to give you honest help when choosing investments, how to choose the best companies, and when to exit your positions.

I've pointed out the importance of keeping good records, how to protect your nest egg from everyone, including Uncle Sam, and how to avoid the traps that many beginners fall prey to.

We've learned why it's so important to begin a savings habit early, how compounding over time can produce incredible results, and how just a small amount is needed to attain superior results if properly managed.

We've seen the importance of patience.

I could have produced a 450 page volume if I thought it would help you. I have always felt that most investing books and manuals were only about 10% helpful materials and 90% unnecessary fluff.

Like any good poet, I've tried to put as much meaning into each chapter as I could, without overwhelming beginners with the fine details most authors seem to think important. If you keep your investing life simple, have the patience to allow time to do its work, and be suspicious of outrageous claims, you will have the time for the more important aspects of life: family, friends, and your own peace of mind.

If you know someone who's starting out in life, there's nothing better you could do for their financial future than give them a copy of *Investing for Smarties*. Good luck.

GLOSSORY

1099 Form. A form sent to investor and the Internal Revenue Service each year, detailing an individal's or company's financial activity for the year.

Ask. The price for which a security can be purchased.

Bear market. A long duration of falling prices for any items.

Bid. The price buyers will pay for a security

Blow-off phase. The usual result of a feeding frenzy; uncontrolled upward momentum in price.

Bond. A promissory instrument to pay back a specified amount of money at a specified time at a specified rate of interest.

Board of Directors. A group of individuals who oversee the performance of the corporation and sets corporate policy. They also select the CEO. Board members are selected by the shareholders.

Broker. A company of individual who transacts buy and sells of investments for a commission.

Bull market. A long duration of rising prices for any items.

Buying long. To order a specific number of securities anticipating a rise in share price in order to profit.

Capitalization. The total amount of capital available to a company derived from selling shares to investors.

Chief Executive Officer (CEO). The individual whose job it is to carry out the company's policies, to make a positive contribution to allow the company to flourish.

Chief Governance Officer (CGO). An individual in a corporation whose responsibility it is to protect the shareholders, making sure management is being fair and honest.

Corporation. An organization formed by individuals for the purpose of raising capital, by selling shares to investors, for the purpose of developing or expanding the corporation's activities.

Equity. Stocks.

Feeding frenzy. A time when investors will bid up a security way beyond its fair value.

Governance. A measurement of how well a company performs its duties towards protecting its shareholders

Index Fund. A mutual fund that sells shares to buy a specific group of companies such as The Dow Jones Industrial, or the S & P 500. At recent count, there were 140 index funds.

Individual Retirement Account (IRA). A personal retirement account which allows individuals to set aside part of their retirement funds tax-deferred.

Institutional investors. Large investment organizations such as mutual funds, banks, and retirement plans.

Keogh Plan. Allows self-employed individuals to save a portion of their income for retirement tax-deferred.

Large-capitalization companies. Companies with over $12 billion capitalization.

Market, The. Phrase used to describe the total stock market, of which there are many segments.

Money Market Fund. A mutual fund that sells shares in order to buy short-term, high quality securities.

Mid-capitalization companies (mid-cap). Companies with capitalization between $1 billion and $12 billion.

Mutual Fund. An investment firm that offers shares of the fund to the investing public. The fund then buys investments using the monies realized from those sales.

New York Stock Exchange. The largest stock and bond exchange in the United States. Their job is to bring together buyers and sellers. They handle over 3,000 different securities and more than 2,000 bonds. Also known as The Big Board.

Order, Good 'til Cancelled. An order to buy or sell a security and to stay in effect until filled or cancelled by the customer.

Order, limit. An order to buy or sell any security at a stipulated price. Commissions are usually higher for limit orders.

Order, market. An order to buy or sell any security as quickly as possible with no price specified.

Order, open. See Order, good-'til-cancelled.

Roth IRA. A federally-approved individual retirement account which allows individuals to set aside a portion of their income towards retirement. Any contributions are not tax-deductible, as with conventional IRAs, but all earnings are tax-free, even when withdrawn. There are restrictions on maximum earnings to quality and on how much can be contributed annually.

Sector. A group of companies basically in the same business activity.

Securities and Exchange Commission (SEC). The federal agency that administers U.S. securities laws.

Security. An instrument that proves ownership in a company or shows a creditor relationship with a company or any government agency. Securities include stock shares, bonds, and real estate.

Self-directed IRA. A retirement plan which allows participants to buy and sell securities, usually through a brokerage account.

Selling short. The process whereby an investor temporarily borrows stock or commodities in anticipation of profiting from a lower price of the security in the future. The difference between the short sell and the price of the buy is the profit. One sells to short and buys to get out of the position, hopefully for a profit. *See also Buying long.*

Share. A single unit of ownership in a corporation of mutual fund.

Small capitalization companies (Small cap). Companies capitalized at $1 billion or less. Usually newly developed or start-up businesses with not much history to research.

Stock. An ownership share of a corporation

Stop loss, trailing. An order placed below a security's current price to sell if the price should fall, and conversely, to buy if the price rises on a short position. Both are used to protect capital if the market moves against your position.

Ticker. A reporting system where the latest prices on securities are reported.

Ticker symbol. The ticker identification for a security.

Volume. The total number of transactions occurring during a given time on any individual exchange.

ANNOTATED BIBLIOGRAPHY

Anonymous and Timothy Harper. *License to Steal: The Secret World of Wall Street and the Systematic Plundering of the American Investor*. New York: HarperBusiness, 1999.

This is an excellent report that will help you understand how brokers manipulate their clients in order to prosper.

Attarian, John. "The Myth of the Social Security 'Trust Fund'". http://www.libertyhaven.com/politicsandcurrentevents/ healthcarewelfareorsocialsecurity/mythsocial.shtml

Explains that there is no trust fund, and why the government's own pub-lic-relations efforts are the source of the misunderstanding.

Baer, Gregory and Gary Gensler. *The Great Mutual Fund Trap: An Investment Recovery Plan*. New York: Broadway Books, 2002.

The authors offer an in-depth history of how mutual funds managers have hoodwinked the investing public.

Cole, Benjamin Mark. *The Pied Pipers of Wall Street: How Analysts Sell You Down the River*. Princeton: Bloomberg Press, 2001.

Cole explains how and why Wall Street analysts have sold out the investing public in order to prosper themselves.

Downing, Neil. *The New IRAs and How to Make Them Work for You*. Chicago: Dearborn Trade Publishing, 2002.

This is a good reference on how IRAs work and how to use them.

Dempsey, Mark. *Tricks of the Trade: An Insider's Guide to Using a Stockbroker.* Indianapolis: Park Avenue, 1998.

The author, a former broker, relates his experiences, showing how brokers manipulate their clients in order to fill quotas and generate better commissions.

Elder, Alexander. *Come Into My Trading Room: A Complete Guide to Trading.* New York: John Wiley & Sons, 2002.

Dr. Elder's book is for advanced learning. He gives many good ideas about how to organize your time and effort, keeping good records, selecting markets and designing a money-making tree. You'll gain many insights from his twenty years of trading and teaching.

Investing Made Easy: Select Works from Investor's Business Daily's Investor's Corner. Los Angeles: Investor's Business Daily, Inc. 2002.

This selection is an important tool to help in understanding the workings of the market.

Investor's Business Daily (IBD). Los Angeles: Investor's Business Daily, Inc., 1991–.

A daily financial newspaper whose policy is to report accurate information on every aspect of investing. They do an excellent job of educating the general public on how to invest.

Levitt, Arthur with Paula Dwyer. *Take on the Street: What Wall Street and Corporate America Don't Want You to Know: What You Can Do to Fight Back.* New York: Pantheon Books, 2002.

Mr. Levitt speaks to the collapse of the system for overseeing our capital markets. He addresses some of the more flagrant abuses that companies, mutual funds, analysts, accountants, and brokerage houses perpetrate against the investing community.

O'Neil, William J. *How to Make Money in Stocks: A Winning System in Good Times or Bad.* 3d ed. New York: McGraw-Hill, 2002.

> This very important book should be your investing bible. Mr. O'Neil traces back to 1953 to show you how to minimize risk, maximize return, and find stocks poised to perform.

Orman, Suze. *The Road to Wealth: A Comprehensive Guide to Your Money.* New York: Riverhead Books, 2001.

> Ms. Orman addresses many aspects of wealth building. With a question and answer format, the author gives clear, easy to understand definitions of almost every term you encounter in investing.

Rothchild, John. *A Fool and His Money: The Odyssey of an Average Investor.* New York: John Wiley & Sons, 1997.

> This is light reading which mostly shows you how not to invest.

Scott, David L. *Wall Street Words: An Essential A to Z Guide for Today's Investor.* Boston: Houghton Mifflin, 1997.

> This is a helpful reference of financial definitions and useful tips.

Shiller, Robert J. *Irrational Exuberance.* Princeton: Princeton University Press, 2000.

> Copyrighted just before the high tech bubble burst, the author warns of excessive stock prices being on shaky ground. Shiller offers eye-opening information to help investors recognize when the market is overpriced.

Sloan, Allan. "Fuzzy Math" http://msnbc.msn.com/id/6724252/site/newsweek/

> The columnist claims that there's no accounting for the new Social Security plan—the one that calls for partially privatizing individual accounts.

"Social Security Trust Fund" from *Wikipedia, the Free Encyclopedia*. http://
en.wikipedia.org/wiki/Social_Security_Trust_Fund

Explains how the fund was originally set up and how it operates today.

Stav, Julie with Deborah Adamson. *Get Your Share: The Everyday Woman's
Guide to Striking It Rich in the Stock Market*. New York: Berkley Books,
2000.

Writing for women, the author suggests, in a clear fashion, how to get
started investing. She places emphasis on investing clubs.

Tanner, Michael. "Pointless Debate over Social Security Trust Fund". http://
www.cato.org/cgi–bin/scripts/printtech.cgi/dailys/10–16–99.html

This short article argues in favor of privatization, taking Social Security
completely out of the hands of politicians.

Value Line. New York: Value Line, 1998–.

An excellent guide to help select companies that will perform the best in
the coming six to twelve months. Available at most libraries or by subscription.

Wolman, William and Anne Colamosca. *The Great 401(k) Hoax: Why Your
Family's Financial Security Is at Risk, and What You Can Do About It*.
Cambridge: Perseus Publishing, 2002.

If you are presently investing using a 401(k), this book can help you
investigate the manner in which it is being managed. It includes methods for receiving the best results.

WEBOGRAPHY

www.investors.com
This is the IBD site. It offers research, articles, workshops, and news.

www.investapedia.com
This is a great resource. It is a investment dictionary/encyclopedia containing articles, tutorials, and a trading simulator.

www.investmentu.com
At this site you can sign up for a twice-weekly email newsletter.

www.morningstar.com
Here you will find articles, workshops, newsletters, analysis, and more.

www2.standardandpoors.com
Includes news, research, and indices.

www.valueline.com
The mission statement states that "our mission is to help investors get the most accurate and independently created research information available, in any format they choose, and teach them how to use it to meet their financial objectives."

INDEX

978-0-595-39077-9
0-595-39077-3

www.ingramcontent.com/pod-product-compliance
Lightning Source LLC
Chambersburg PA
CBHW030907180526
45163CB00004B/1745